Go Vegan – Save Your Life

Non-Preachy, Non-Judgy Beginners Guide to a Plant-Based Diet and Cruelty-Free Living

Victoria Simmons

Table of Contents

Introduction: Welcome to the Book Which Will Save Your Life!

Are you a vegan? Are you thinking about becoming a vegan? Or are you a die-hard meat-lover who just wants to learn more about veganism? No matter where you are in your veganism journey, reading this book may save your life!

Right now, how much do you know about vegan life?

For sure, you may have heard this term already. You may have also asked around about how it's like to be a vegan, especially from your vegan acquaintances, friends, and family members. But do you really know what it means to be a vegan? If not, read on! Even if you are already familiar with veganism, this book will provide you with a lot of insights which may help convince you to take that courageous step to change your life for the better.

Although a lot of people want to make a change to veganism, there are a lot of reasons which are holding them back. Aside from learning more about being a vegan, we will also be going through these reasons and some helpful advice on how to overcome them. Basically, this book is for vegans, people who are leaning towards plant-based eating, people who have started their veganism journey but are struggling, or those who are just curious but open-minded about the vegan lifestyle.

After reading this book, you can apply the knowledge and strategies to your own life in order to take that first step into this healthy and beneficial lifestyle. Even if you've been a vegan for some time now, this book can help refresh your knowledge about veganism and keep you motivated to stick with the lifestyle you have chosen for yourself.

Just like any other journey in life, veganism comes with its own challenges. But the good news is that with enough encouragement, will, and motivation, you can stick with your decision and enjoy the long-term benefits in the future!

One thing you shouldn't expect from this book is for me to speak from a meat eater's perspective. I am a vegan, I'm proud to be one, and I would like to share everything I've learned along the way. So even if you take a step or two back, don't worry about feeling bad. Veganism is all about listening to your needs, your body, and your values. With that being said, let's begin!

Chapter 1: Myth Busting

One of the main reasons why people are reluctant to go

vegan is because there are SO MANY myths surrounding veganism. Although there is no truth to these myths, a lot of people still believe them, especially when they hear them from people whom they know and trust. So, if you want to become a vegan, you must start learning the truth about this healthy lifestyle choice.

This chapter is all about myth busting. Here are the most common myths circulating out there and the truths behind them. The more you learn about veganism, the more you can make an informed decision on whether you should start becoming one or not. Then you can start sharing the truth about veganism to others in order to help out in your own way.

Myth 1 - All vegans are Weirdos and Hippies

This is one of those myths which makes us vegans roll our eyes (admit it, if you're a vegan, you probably rolled your eyes too!). Sure, this may have been somewhat true about 40 or 50 years ago, but today, this is nothing but a myth! Today, vegans exist among all professions, ages, cultures, genders, and nations. You can see us everywhere, and most of us are neither hippies (there's nothing wrong with being a hippie though) nor weirdos. There are even a lot of celebrities who have already chosen to become vegan! Some of these vegan celebrities include:

- **Ellen Page**, a longtime vegan who isn't afraid to speak to the public about the reasons for her lifestyle choice.

- **Alicia Silverstone**, a vegan who also happens to be an animal lover.

- **Ariana Grande** who firmly believes that a plant-based, whole-food diet can help everyone live longer and healthier lives.

- **Ellen DeGeneres,** who is a very outspoken animal advocate and who has the power and drive to bring awareness of veganism to a mainstream audience.

- **Joaquin Phoenix** who has been a vegan since he was 3 years old and who has encouraged a lot of other celebrities to become vegans too.

These are just a few vegan Hollywood celebs you should know about. Other big names include Miley Cyrus, Liam Hemsworth, Woody Harrelson, Mayim Bialik, Casey Affleck, Sia, Stevie Wonder, Pamela Anderson, Peter Dinklage, James Cameron, and so on.

Myth 2 - Veganism is Difficult and Expensive

A lot of people believe this so they think that they can't really afford to become vegans. But when you think about it, veganism isn't that different from other diets. We all have to buy ingredients for dishes, order meals at restaurants, and purchase food items for our snacks.

But as long as you don't go for the "fancy stuff," being a vegan is actually a lot cheaper! For instance, if you're worried about spending too much on meals at restaurants, then eat most of your meals at home and only dine out on special occasions. When it's time to start shopping for food, shop smart!

Purchase fruits and vegetables which are in season. Whole grains and legumes come at a reasonable price. If you want to include seeds and nuts in your diet, go for the shelled variety as these are a lot cheaper. It's all about knowing what to buy when you're on a budget.

Myth 3 - Veganism is Just a New Trend

The 1st of November is World Vegan Day, and this healthy lifestyle has been around since the year 1944. Although the term "veganism" was coined in that year, people in the ancient Eastern Mediterranean and Indian societies have been practicing the concept of veganism. If you need more proof of this, even Gandhi mentioned veganism in his teachings.

Famous as Gandhi was, this part of his life isn't really emphasized. This is probably because most of those who live in India are vegans and vegetarians anyway. So maybe it was just assumed that he was one too. But for Gandhi, he made this lifestyle choice consciously, and his reason was ethical in nature.

In his younger years, Gandhi experimented by eating meat. But then he gave this up in an attempt to please his mother. Then when he studied in England, he came across a pamphlet by Henry Salt, which changed his life. He then made it his mission to spread the word to the rest of the world.

Gandhi had a genuine concern for animals. When he spoke about nonviolence, he also referred to animals. Although he did consume goat's milk, he never ate meat. In fact, he even said that if he should perish unless he takes mutton or beef-tea, even if the advice came from medical professionals, he would prefer death!

Myth 4 - Animals are Here for Us to Eat

Again, maybe this may have been true in the past, like back when our ancestors had no choice but to eat the flesh of animals. But can we really say this with conviction today when we have so many options available to us?

These days we have WholeFoods, Walmart, farmer's markets, and other local shops where there are endless choices of fresh, whole, and vegan-friendly food options. When it comes to plant-based sources, there are so many options available. Therefore, we don't have to eat animals to survive!

Although we all believe different things, I've found a few bible verses which can help debunk this particular myth right now. If you're not really a believer in religion, that's okay! But when you try to process these verses, you'll see that they do make a lot of sense.

Right after he created the world, God said, "I give you every seed-bearing plant on the face of the whole earth and every tree that has fruit with seed in it. They will be yours for food. And to all the beasts of the earth and all the birds of the air and all the creatures that move on the ground – everything that has the breath of life in it – I give every green plant for food. And it was so." (Genesis

1:29-30)

See? I told you this was an excellent verse to prove this point.

If you believe in God and the words of the Bible, you can see how the world He created was a vegan world, not one where we should go around eating the animals which live in it.

Myth 5 - Vegans are Often Sick and Weak

The truth is actually the opposite of this myth. As William Clifford Roberts, MD stated in The American Journal of Cardiology, 'When we kill animals to eat, they end up killing us because their flesh, which contains cholesterol and saturated fat, was never intended for human beings, who are natural herbivores.' [1]

If you plan your plant-based diet well, you can enjoy a lot of health benefits. One such benefit is the anti-inflammatory effect of the foods often associated with a vegan diet. Therefore, when you follow a vegan diet,

---

[1] Retrieved from https://www.ajconline.org/article/0002-9149(90)90383-C/pdf

which reduces the inflammation in your body, this makes you less vulnerable for different kinds of illnesses.

In one particular study, researchers studied the effects of the different types of diets in terms of the outcomes of diseases and health (Tai Le & Sabate, Beyond Meatless, the Health Effects of Vegan Diets: Findings from the Adventist Cohorts, 2014). Through this study, the researchers found out that vegan and vegetarian diets had significant positive effects on diseases such as type-2 diabetes, metabolic syndrome, some types of cancer, and more.

This study and others like it show how the vegan diet can help you become healthier and stronger too. Veganism has a lot of long-term health benefits, which is why more and more people are starting to follow this lifestyle.

Myth 6 - Vegans Don't Get Enough Calcium

This is one of the biggest concerns non-vegans have, which makes them feel reluctant about going vegan. Since vegans don't consume dairy products, how would they get enough calcium? While growing up, most of us have been told over and over that we should drink milk in order to make our bones strong. I really believed this advice told to me by my own mother, and it really pushed me to finish each glass of milk each and every day.

That is until I learned more about plant-based eating and became a vegan myself. The truth is, we don't just get calcium from milk and other dairy products. Think about all those strong animals who only survive on plants such as horses, camels, gorillas, elephants, donkeys, cows, and so on. They eat grass and plants all day, every day and yet, they don't seem to be calcium deficient. So how does this happen?

It's because these herbivores eat a lot of plants! Therefore, you can also get all the calcium you need from different plant-based sources. These are healthier than cheese, meat, and other animal-based calcium sources because, over time, these sources will start making your body more acidic. Then your body will start using up the calcium you have accumulated just to neutralize the adverse effects of acidity. It's a vicious cycle which you can avoid by sticking with plants!

Myth 7 - You Can't Perform Sports if You Don't Eat Meat

Just like calcium, you can get all the protein you need from plants when you follow a vegan diet. And I'm not talking about incomplete proteins either. There are a lot of plant-based sources which contain complete proteins meaning all of the 20 essential amino acids. When it comes to these amino acids, we only require a specific amount of each daily. Dietitians have confirmed that plant-based food sources contain varying amino acid profiles, which means that us vegans are guaranteed to get our required daily dose without much effort.

What does this have to do with performing sports?

Well, in order to perform well in sports, you must consume sufficient amounts of proteins. To illustrate this more clearly, let's see what science has to say. There was one study which focused on training while supplementing with pea protein versus whey protein (Babault, et al., Pea proteins oral supplementation promotes muscle thickness gains during resistance training: a double-blind, randomized, Placebo-controlled clinical trial vs. Whey protein, 2015). By the end of the study, the researchers concluded that there wasn't any significant difference between the groups who used either one of the protein supplementation options. This means that pea protein is just as effective as whey protein. This study was conducted on a group of 161 males who were aged between 18-35 years old who underwent 12 weeks of resistance training on the muscles of their upper limbs.

If this study isn't enough to convince you, there are a lot of vegan athletes out there who are always performing at their best even while taking their proteins and other nutrients from plant-based food sources. Some of the more famous ones include Venus Williams, Tony Gonzales, David Haye, Laura Dennis, Mac Danzig, Mike Tyson, John Salley, Jake Shields, Meagan Duhamel, and the list goes on!

Myth 8 - All Plant-Based Foods are Healthy

Here's one myth that also serves as a precaution to all the vegans and would-be vegans out there. Just because a certain food item is derived from plants, this doesn't necessarily mean that it's healthy. There are certain adulterated foods such as chips, sugar, pre-packaged foods, and sugary drinks, which may be completely plant-based but aren't good for you.

Part of being a vegan is also knowing which kinds of foods are healthy for you. Otherwise, you would be defeating your own purpose for going vegan in order to live a healthier lifestyle. If you have the time, you should always opt for meals which you have prepared from raw fruits, vegetables, and other whole foods. Do this if you want to remain healthy and strong while following your vegan diet.

Myth 9 - If Everybody Goes Vegan, We Won't Have Enough Land to Grow Plants

There are different reasons why people choose to become vegan. But what do you think would happen if everyone in the whole world makes this choice? If this happens by some miracle, there may also be some drawbacks affecting a significant percentage of the population.

Just because I'm a vegan and I encourage others to choose this lifestyle too, it doesn't mean that I don't acknowledge the possible downsides as well. Veganism will be highly beneficial for developed countries, particularly in terms of health and the environment. But for the countries which are still in the process of development, there may be some adverse effects in terms of poverty.

Although if the entire world goes vegan overnight, it would stave off around 8 million deaths each year. Such a situation would lead to a reduction in global mortality by about 10%, and we would see a 60% drop in food-related emissions. While there's a very low likelihood of the whole world suddenly choosing to go vegan, this change is now happening for a lot of people.

But would we have enough land to grow our plants on if this happens?

The fact is, the diet of meat-eaters requires 14x more water, 10x more energy, and 17x more land than the diet of vegans. Most of these resources are used for growing crops to feed the animals instead of us humans. With these numbers, you can see that there would be enough land for us to grow our food on in case we all decide to become vegans.

Myth 10 - Meat is Necessary to Have a Balanced Diet

What exactly should a balanced diet consist of? If you want to follow a balanced diet, you must get sufficient amounts of water, fat, carbohydrates, protein, minerals, and vitamins. But the fact is, we can get all of these from plants, so we don't really need meat in our diet.

Don't believe me? Here are some examples for you:

- **Plant-based protein sources** include nuts, lentils, tofu, tempeh, quinoa, chickpeas, and peas.

- **Plant-based carbohydrate sources** include potatoes, leafy greens, bulgur, sweet potatoes, brown rice, and other vegetables.

- **Plant-based healthy fat sources** include

avocado, coconut, seeds, and nuts.

As for the other vitamins, minerals, and nutrients, you can get these from these plant-based sources along with several others which we haven't mentioned. Oftentimes, vegans supplement their diets with vitamin B12. You can do this too unless you are able to consume a lot of fortified foods which contain this essential vitamin. So, this is another myth which we have successfully debunked.

Myth 11 - If You're Single and Go Vegan, Your Dating Life is Ruined

When it comes to dating, this all depends on you. You may choose to only go out with vegans, but you will just end up cutting your dating prospects significantly. Of course, you can also choose to date people who you find genuinely interesting, those you have things in common with, and those who you see having a future with, whether they're vegans or not.

Personally, I choose the latter. There's nothing wrong with dating a non-vegan as long as you both accept each other's lifestyle. I learned that it's better to say that you're vegan from the get-go. That way, you can see how the other person reacts and whether your lifestyle choice is a deal breaker. Also, you don't have to stop being vegan just so people will go out with you.

Chapter 2: Where Do You Get Your Protein?

If you're planning to go vegan, prepare yourself for a lot of questions your family, friends, and the other people in your life will ask. And when they ask you these questions, they will expect you to know all the answers. One of the more common questions to expect from non-vegans is, "Where do you get your protein?"

For some reason, there is an obsession with protein. In this modern world, it's hard NOT to be obsessed with protein because it's one of the essential nutrients we need to stay at the peak of our health. There's no doubt about it; we need enough protein. I used to believe that I can only get protein from meat.

Have you ever wondered how much protein you need each day? Generally, this varies from one person to another. One way to find out is to take your weight in pounds then multiply this by 0.4. This calculation gives you an idea of how many grams of protein your body requires each day. Of course, this is a subjective method of trying to determine the amount of protein you need. If you want to be sure, consult with a dietitian or with your doctor.

Although we're all obsessed with proteins, it's actually very difficult to become deficient in this macronutrient. As a matter of fact, very few people would fall short of their daily protein requirement, making them protein deficient. Usually, this is because they suffer from some type of eating disorder.

As a vegan, it's easy to meet your RDA for protein. This is because most types of seeds, nuts, grains, beans, and vegetables are high in protein. There was even a large study conducted where they came up with a comparison of the nutrient profiles of vegans and vegetarians (Rizzo, et al., Nutrient profiles of vegetarian and nonvegetarian dietary patterns, 2013). Through this study, the researchers discovered that on average, vegans are able to consume roughly 70% more than the daily protein recommendation.

In the case of athletes who need more protein to stay fit while they're training, they can still perform well even while following a vegan diet. We have mentioned a few names of vegan athletes in the previous chapter. If you have followed the careers of these athletes, you would know that their performance wasn't compromised just because of their diet and lifestyle choice. To guide you, here are some of the best possible protein sources you can consume on a vegan diet:

- **Seeds, nuts, and nut butter**

These are some excellent protein sources to keep on-hand, especially if you're always on-the-go or if you love snacking.

- **Tofu**

  This is another excellent protein source as it contains nine essential amino acid. It's a classic vegan staple that works well in different kinds of meals and it happens to be my favorite protein-rich food for savory wok dishes.

- **Legumes and beans**

  These are highly versatile protein sources too. Aside from being high in protein, they also contain B vitamins and fiber.

- **Lentils and chickpeas**

  You can use these great protein sources in different dishes, and they're also great for digestion. I make burgers from chickpeas and vegan meatloaf from lentils. Aside from this, they can also help reduce the bad bacteria in your intestines.

- **Nutritional yeast**

  Also called "nooch," this amazing protein source can be sprinkled over basically anything from mac and cheese to popcorn and more. I like to use it to make a tasty vegan cheese sauce!

- **Tempeh**

    This is a traditional and staple ingredient commonly found in Indonesia. Aside from being rich in protein, this delicious soy-based food is also rich in iron, manganese, and calcium.

- **Vegan meats**

    Finally, there are a lot of vegan meat products available out there which contain protein as well. You can opt for these if you're craving the taste of meat without having to eat actual meat (this may happen, especially for those who have just started their vegan journey).

Ideas for Adding Plant-Based Protein Food Items to Your Meals

Whether you've chosen to go vegan because of health or ethical reason, you must make sure that you always have a balanced diet (maybe except for the occasional cheat day). A balanced diet means that it must contain sufficient amounts of vitamins, minerals, carbohydrates, healthy fats, and, of course, protein. Following such a diet means that you won't be deficient in any of the essential nutrients.

As you plan your meals, make sure that each meal always contains a food source that's rich in protein. If not, you might end up only eating meals full of carbohydrates and nothing much else while calling them "vegan meals."

This is never a good idea. Remember that starting a vegan lifestyle is already a huge change as it is. Because of your new diet, your body will start undergoing changes which might make you feel out of sorts. Of course, this doesn't mean that you should stop. This is just your body's way of telling you that it's adjusting to the changes.

Since this chapter is all about protein, the all-essential macronutrient, let me give you some ideas for adding more plant-based protein sources to your daily meals:

- If you enjoy smoothies, try adding pumpkin protein when you prepare them. Pumpkin protein has a very plain taste making it an excellent combination with different kinds of plant milk and fresh fruits. For this, each serving contains around 15 grams of protein.

- If you're craving for a snack, try spreading some almond butter on slices of rye bread then sprinkle them with pomegranate seeds or strawberry slices. This is a quick and tasty snack you'll surely enjoy. One serving of this snack contains about 17 grams of protein.

- If you're planning to have a salad for lunch, add a

handful of cooked quinoa to it. This gives you a nutritious, fresh, and filling meal, which contains about 15 grams of protein just for the quinoa.

- Adding raw almonds to your bowl of oatmeal or your plate of salad provides you with up to 7 grams of added protein.

- A scrumptious and warming bowl of stew with lentils contains about 18 grams of protein for each serving.

- If you're having vegan ramen, try adding tofu and pak choi to it. This increases the protein content up to 10 grams.

- While you're watching your TV shows, snack on celery and carrot sticks dipped in hummus to get around 10 grams for each serving.

- Change things up by having a bowl of buckwheat for breakfast or by using buckwheat flour to make gluten-free pancakes. For this, each serving would contain around 6 grams of protein.

- Adding soy to your diet is made easy as it comes in many different forms including firm tofu which contains around 10 grams of protein per serving, tempeh which contains around 15 grams of protein per serving, natto which contains around 15 grams of protein per serving, and more.

Chapter 3: The Standard American Diet or "SAD"

A lot of people may not be aware of this, but they are following a diet known as the "Standard American Diet" or SAD. Basically, this is the diet of those who aren't really following any kind of specific diet for any specific purpose.

To help you understand this more, let's discuss what the Standard American Diet is all about. Then you can see if you've been following this diet without you even knowing it. The more you learn about SAD, the more you'll understand why it's not the healthiest diet out there.

What is the Standard American Diet?

The Standard American Diet or SAD is a very common diet which includes a lot of trans fats, saturated fats, excess sugar, refined carbohydrates, and all those other unhealthy things. It's one of the main causes of diabetes and obesity in the US alone. Although this "American style diet" started in the US, the eating pattern has already spread all over the world thus, contributing to the rise of diabetes, obesity, and a wealth of related conditions all around the world.

Even if you're not overweight or obese, this diet causes inflammation directly on the body. It also promotes the development or the worsening of these conditions. Several studies have shown the link between specific components of the SAD and a wide range of medical conditions:

- The high saturated fat content of this diet elevates the levels of cholesterol.

- The high sugar and refined white flour contents of this diet elevate the levels of serum triglycerides.

- The high processed food contents this diet increases the risk of developing depression.

- The high processed and cured red meats contents of this diet increase the risk of developing colon cancer.

With all of these scary effects of this diet, you can see why veganism is a better choice, right?

There's a reason why this diet is abbreviated as "SAD"

Although the US is one of the most well-developed and prosperous countries in the world, most of its citizens tend to die sooner or experience more diseases compared to the citizens of other, less-developed countries.

And this is all because of the Standard American Diet. This diet is abbreviated as "SAD" for a reason. To give you a better idea of what it contains, here's a breakdown of what this diet contains:

- 63% of the calories are taken from processed and refined foods such as potato chips, soft drinks, packaged desserts, and more.

- 25% of the calories are taken from animal-based food sources.

- 12% of the calories are taken from plant-based food sources.

Sure, 12% seems reasonable, but most of the time, half of this comes from unhealthy plant-based food sources such as French fries, vegetable chips, and the like. Therefore, this means that only around 6% of the calories are taken from whole foods which promote health. The abbreviation of this diet suits it perfectly because it also leads to Standard American Diseases which, in turn, lead to Standard American Deaths!

In order to stop this diet from causing more and more deaths around the country and the world, it's time to make a change. Starting your vegan journey is an excellent step towards your health.

The effects of following this diet

The more you follow the Standard American Diet, it would be like you're eating yourself to death. This may seem like an exaggeration or a painful truth, but it's something more of us must realize and take to heart. Several studies have shown how SAD plays a significant role in the development of a number of diseases. Also, if you're already suffering from these diseases, continuously following this diet may aggravate your condition.

Sad as this fact is (no pun intended!), we have to face the reality that the SAD is the unhealthiest diet you can ever follow in your life. Let's take a look at the long-term effects this diet causes:

- **Obesity**

  This is one of the most common effects of this disease. It's bad enough to be overweight. But when you're obese, this will increase your risk of different kinds of illnesses and disorders. The more obese you are, the higher your risk becomes. So, you may want to re-think your diet and consider healthier alternatives.

- **Diabetes**

  Nowadays, type-2 diabetes is almost being considered an epidemic. This is one of the most common diseases which develops when you're obese. Unfortunately, it's a lifelong condition with no treatment. So, if you are diagnosed with diabetes, the best you can do is learn how to live with the condition and manage its symptoms.

- **Stroke**

  This refers to a group of disorders which occur when your blood supply to any part of your brain gets interrupted. The symptoms of stroke vary depending on which part of the brain is affected. However, this has the potential to be fatal, which is why it's extremely dangerous.

- **Coronary artery disease**

  This occurs when there is an accumulation of plaque in the arteries of the heart from mechanical trauma, calcium, or cholesterol. When this happens, it can cause a wide range of effects, the most dangerous of which is a reduced flow of nutrients and oxygen to the muscles of the heart.

- **Gallbladder and kidney disorders**

  These disorders are very serious, especially when they start disrupting the functions of your kidneys. They're painful, debilitating, and may prove fatal when left untreated or unchecked.

The bottom line is this; it's an unhealthy diet which you should definitely stop following as soon as possible. Instead, choose a healthier lifestyle which will make you feel better and which will promote your overall well-being.

Chapter 4: Alkalinity and Acidity

As I've mentioned in the myth-busting chapter, just because you're following a vegan diet, that doesn't mean that you're eating healthy foods. So, what does this have to do with alkalinity and acidity? In the first place, what do these terms mean and why are they important?

Well, when it comes to maintaining your health, you must make sure that your body is alkaline, not acidic. Otherwise, you might start experiencing some negative side effects the more acid your body becomes. Before going into this further, let's first define alkalinity and acidity in terms of diets.

Defining Alkaline and Acidic Diets

The basis of an alkaline diet is the idea that when you replace the "acidic" foods you eat with "alkaline" food items, this can help improve your overall health. Those who follow this diet even claim that such a diet can help combat a wide range of diseases. The alkaline diet, which is also called the alkaline ash diet, or the acid-alkaline diet can help change the pH levels of your body.

You can compare your metabolism to fire. It involves a chemical reaction which breaks down the foods you consume. But unlike fire, your metabolism occurs in a controlled and gradual manner. When you burn something, it leaves as ash as residue. In the same way, the foods you consume also leave a residue which is called "metabolic waste."

This metabolic waste can either be acidic or alkaline, and it can have a direct effect on the acidity of your body. This means that if you eat a lot of acidic foods, your body will be left with acidic ash which, in turn, elevates the acidity level of your blood. But if you eat foods which promote alkalinity, this would make your blood alkaline too.

Unfortunately, the acidic residue can make you more susceptible to diseases and illnesses. Conversely, the alkaline residue can help protect your body. When you consume more alkaline foods, this can help improve your overall health. Some types of foods which leave an acidic residue are those which contain phosphate, sulfur, and protein. Some types of foods which leave an alkaline residue are those which contain potassium, calcium, and magnesium.

There are specific food groups which are considered alkaline, neutral, and acidic. These are:

- **Alkaline:** vegetables, fruits, nuts, and legumes.

- **Acidic:** alcohol, grains, dairy, poultry, eggs, fish, and meat.

As you can see, vegan foods are classified as alkaline foods. However, you must still choose wisely when it comes to the foods you put into your body.

Why does pH matter?

Water is the most abundant compound in our body. The body has its own acid-base or acid-alkaline ratio known as the pH. This refers to the balance between acid-forming or positively charged ions and alkaline-forming or negatively-charged ions. Our body is always striving to maintain a balanced pH in order to prevent the occurrence of health issues.

It's important to maintain the proper pH levels in the body. When your body is acidic, this makes it the best environment for cancer and for other kinds of diseases. Cancer cells thrive in such an acidic body, which is why you should try to avoid acid-forming foods as much as possible.

If you continue to consume acid-forming foods and beverages, a condition known as acidosis may develop. This is a very common issue, especially for those who follow the Standard American Diet. Acidosis occurs when the lungs and kidneys aren't able to maintain the pH balance of the body. Unfortunately, a lot of the normal processes of the body produce acid.

Under normal conditions, the kidneys and lungs may compensate for any minimal imbalances. But when acid starts accumulating in the body, these organs can't keep up which, in turn, leads to more health problems. If you want to correct this condition and bring back the proper pH levels of your body, the best thing you can do is to make a change in your diet and lifestyle.

The benefits of an alkaline diet

Since the vegan diet consists mainly of alkaline foods, does this mean that you will never get cancer? One recent study conducted by Oxford University focused on how our diets affect the risk of developing cancer (Key et al., Vegetarian diets and the incidence of cancer in a low-risk population, 2014). This study showed that vegans have a significantly lower risk of developing this disease. The study ran for 15 years, and it involved 60,000 women and men from Britain. More than 18,000 of these participants were vegetarians while around 2,200 of them were vegan. Through the study, the researchers found out that the overall incidence of cancer compared to those who ate meat was 19% lower in vegans and 11% lower in vegetarians.

In another study, this time which involved 70,000 participants, the researchers focused on the incidence of cancer and on the dietary patterns of those involved (Tantamango-Bartley, et. al., Cancer in British vegetarians: updated analyses of 4998 incident cancers in a cohort of 32,491 meat eaters, 8612 fish eaters, 18,298 vegetarians, and 2246 vegans, 2013). The results of this study suggested that the vegan diet is associated with a lower risk of developing different types of cancers compared to non-vegans.

Since the vegan diet allows you to consume more alkaline foods, this helps maintain healthy pH levels in your body. Here are some outstanding benefits of following an alkaline vegan diet:

- Consuming more fresh fruits and vegetables improves the K/Na ratio of your body. This may also be beneficial for the health of your bones, in reducing the rate of muscle wasting, and in helping mitigate stroke, hypertension, and other kinds of chronic diseases.

- When you follow an alkaline diet, this results in an increase in essential growth hormones which, in turn, may positively affect a lot of outcomes from cognition to memory and even cardiovascular health.

- An alkaline diet may also increase the intracellular magnesium in your body. This is important for the optimal functioning of several enzyme systems. When your body has available magnesium, which is needed for the activation of vitamin D, this leads to several additional benefits in your vitamin D exocrine and apocrine systems.

- Alkalinity may also provide an added benefit for some kinds of chemotherapeutic agents which require a higher level of pH.

With all these benefits and more, you can see how the vegan diet which promotes alkalinity can help reduce the mortality and morbidity of chronic diseases which are very common in our modern society. Apart from choosing whole, fresh fruits and vegetables, you may also want to find out the type of soil the produce you purchase has been grown in. This is because this may have a significant effect on the mineral contents of these fruits and vegetables.

How to make your diet more alkaline as a vegan?

As time goes by, introducing outside substances to your body changes its pH. Therefore, it should come as no surprise that the quality and kinds of foods you consume will have a significant effect on the acidity of your body. If you keep eating meat, dairy, processed foods, fast foods, excess alcohol, and sugar, this may increase your body's acidity drastically.

Since our bodies are always trying to maintain the proper pH levels, it will start pulling alkalizing minerals from the tissues and organs in order to buffer and to eliminate acid from your system. If this keeps happening, the structures and cells of your body will start falling apart. The good news is that, when you follow a vegan lifestyle, there are many kinds of foods which you can consume to help promote alkalinity. Consider these options:

- **Citrus fruits**

  Although grapefruits, limes, lemons, and other citrus fruits may have an acidic taste, when your body breaks them down, the residue produced is buffering alkaline minerals.

- **Green vegetables**

  These are readily available no matter where you look. Although eating these fresh veggies is always a great way to consume them, you can also press them to create green juice. This liquid form makes the green veggies more effective because it would travel throughout your body more rapidly in order to provide a buffering effect against acidity.

- **Parsley and other green herbs**

Use this as a garnish, as a salad ingredient or even in healthy juices. Parsley is rich in vitamin C, vitamin K, and it offers powerful alkalizing effects since it contains a lot of other minerals.

- **Garlic and onions**

  These veggies absorb different kinds of nutrients as they grow in the soil. If you want the most alkalizing varieties, you may want to choose organic.

These are just some examples of the most alkalizing types of fruits and vegetables you can add to your diet. But the good news is that there are a lot more options for vegans because we basically thrive on alkalizing foods!

Chapter 5: The China Study

Back in the early part of the 1980s, a nutritional biochemist from Cornell University named T. Colin Campbell, Ph.D. partnered up with researchers at the Chinese Academy of Preventive Medicine and at Oxford University. They started one of the most comprehensive studies focused on nutrition, and it was called the China Project. At that time, China offered a unique opportunity to the researchers.

The population of the country had a tendency to live in a single area throughout their lives, and they also had a tendency to follow the same diets according to the region where they resided. Generally, the diets of these people were high in dietary fiber and plant materials while being low in fat. Obviously, these diets were quite the opposite of the rich diets of the countries in the western part of the world. This plant-based nature of the diet of the rural Chinese population gave the researchers an opportunity to compare their plant-based diets with the westerner's animal-based ones.

Sixty-five counties in the rural area of the country were chosen for this study, which focused on their lifestyle, disease, and dietary characteristics. Within each of these counties, the researchers chose two villages where they randomly chose fifty families in each of those villages.

Around 6,500 participants were involved in the survey wherein they were asked to provide food, urine, and blood samples, which were kept for later analysis. Also, the participants answered questionnaires and were asked to provide 3-day diet information which the researchers had recorded.

These samples and information were taken from the participants in 1983-1984. Then the same participants from the same counties were re-surveyed in 1989-1990 along with twenty additional counties in Taiwan and in China's mainland. The researchers added twenty new families from each county, giving them a total of 10,200 new participants. For this second survey, they also collected socioeconomic information from the participants. The data and text from the second survey have already been digitized, making them accessible to the public.

In the early part of the 1990s, the very first results from this study were already being published. Then a documentary crew from Cornell started filming a documentary in the different locations included in the study along with the research facilities in order to capture the significance and the scope of the China Project.

In the year 2005, T. Colin Campbell, Ph.D. along with Thomas M. Campbell, MD, his son, shared the findings of this study along with other research. They authored a bestselling book wherein they examined the connection between nutrition and a wide range of diseases. Until now, the China Study is considered one of the most significant studies about health and diet ever conducted.

What Do the Results of the Study Prove?

The China Study happens to be one of the most significant studies which have been conducted. The book has been talked about quite a lot thanks to all the interesting and significant information it has provided.

Since this book was published, it has inspired and encouraged people all over the world to start their vegan journey. Some of the most influential figures, such as Bill Clinton have read this book and have become vegans because of it. But what do the results of this study prove? We've already talked about the study, now let's go through what the results mean:

- In the study, the researchers have shared a lot of disturbing statistics regarding diabetes, heart disease, and obesity in America (especially when comparing these statistics to those of China). Also, they have discovered that Americans pay more for health care compared to any other country in the world. However, they don't really have better health to show for these higher payments!

- The conclusions made by the researchers are based on a huge amount of data. The participants of this study were actual people, not mice or other lab animals which have been kept in controlled environments. After the study, they were able to collect over 8,000 associations between disease, diet, and lifestyle, which are statistically significant.

- The researchers had discovered that animal protein does, in fact, promote cancer growth. According to the author of the book, they performed several animal studies which were peer-reviewed wherein they found out that they can turn cancer cell growth "on and off" simply by altering the doses of casein, which happens to be the main protein component in cow's milk.

- Rather than worrying about pesticides too much (although you shouldn't ignore these completely), people should worry more about poor nutrition. This is because the food we eat has a direct effect on how our cells interact with carcinogens.

- It's actually possible to reverse heart disease through proper nutrition. This was one conclusion taken from the study, along with other data and information gathered from respected physicians who support the findings.

- Carbohydrates aren't always the enemy as most of us believe. That is to say, when you get your carbohydrates from healthy, whole plant-based sources, these are considered healthy carbs. But the ones you must avoid are the highly processed and refined carbohydrates.

- Cancer isn't the only disease you can avoid by following a plant-based diet. According to research, such a diet can also help you prevent autoimmune diseases, obesity, diabetes, kidney, bone, brain, and eye diseases.

- It's not necessary to "tailor a diet" to target specific benefits. Instead, you should try to aim for a healthy, well-balanced diet which will provide you with several health benefits to support your well-being across the board!

- It's not necessary for us to eat meat. The study showed that there are basically no nutrients you can get from animal-based sources which aren't better provided by plant-based sources.

- The bottom line is this – eating plants makes you healthier. Those who followed animal-based diets had a higher likelihood of developing chronic diseases. While those who followed plant-based diets proved to be the healthiest, whether you plan to go vegan, vegetarian, or you just want to make a change, adding as many plants on your plate will be highly beneficial.

Chapter 6: What if Your Doctor Doesn't Agree?

As a vegan myself, I can say that I had experienced a lot of different reactions when I told people about the choice I made. A lot of times, people have reacted to my big life-decision by asking me, "If veganism is so beneficial, then why doesn't my doctor recommend it?"

This is a legitimate question, of course. After all, we should all listen to our doctors, right. But the fact is, when it comes to your diet, doctors might not be the best people to determine what's good for you since they aren't nutrition specialists. Also, imagine a world where we are all vegan. We'd all be strong, healthy, and free of diseases (assuming that we all go for the healthy vegan food choices). In such a utopic world, who will even have the need for doctors?

What are the Reasons Why Doctors Won't Agree to Let You Go Vegan?

When you try to search for information about vegan and

other plant-based diets on the internet, you will find a wealth of information. You'll learn about the benefits of such diets, and all of these seem to be incredible! So why won't your doctor agree with this choice of yours?

The fact is, doctors, don't really undergo a lot of training in nutrition. Throughout medical school, they may only have a couple of hours dedicated to this subject. Therefore, the information they possess about nutrition may only be as broad as the information of those who have read a lot about nutrition from articles online. And since there are a lot of myths out there, these may have influenced the beliefs of doctors.

Think about the myths we had just debunked in Chapter 1. If your doctor believes these myths, then why would they recommend a vegan diet to you or any other patient? If you want to consult someone about going vegan, the best person to talk to would be a nutrition specialist such a dietitian. That way, you can ask all the questions you want to and feel confident about the answers you will be getting from them.

What Should You Do?

Anyone who has made a choice to go vegan will feel challenged and overwhelmed at one point or another. But this doesn't have to make you quit cold turkey. There are hundreds of thousands of resources available which can help you with your journey, such as this book! The more you learn about the vegan lifestyle, how to start, and how to maintain this lifestyle, the easier it will be for you to stick with your choice.

Just because your doctor doesn't agree with this lifestyle choice, that doesn't make it wrong. At the end of the day, the decision lies with you. If you have done extensive research about veganism, you've spoken to nutritionists and other vegans, and you believe that this is the right choice for you, then, by all means, go for it!

Personally, I have never regretted my decision to become a vegan. Although I've experienced a few challenges along the way, I've also seen and felt the many benefits of this diet and lifestyle choice first-hand. So, if you had the chance to meet and get to know me, I would be one of those people who would encourage you to follow this lifestyle if you think that it would be best for you in the long run.

Chapter 7: Soy – The Misunderstood Superfood

If you're fond of Asian cuisine, you'd know that soy is quite popular. Asians use this ingredient a lot for how it tastes and for the many health benefits it provides. Since being hailed as a "superfood," soy may now become a staple in the US as well. Despite its popularity though, there are still a lot of people feel reluctant to add it to their diets.

In the year 1999, the USFDA allowed soy manufacturers to make a claim that consuming soy protein as part of the diet may help reduce the levels of cholesterol as well as the risk of developing heart disease. In fact, the FDA even recommends consuming up to 25 grams of soy protein each day in order to enjoy these benefits. Soy also has the potential to reduce the risk of developing menopausal symptoms, kidney disease, osteoporosis, Alzheimer's disease, and certain types of cancer.

Why Do People Fear Soy?

Soy is a type of legume which has been cultivated and eaten for centuries by a lot of Asian cultures as a staple. Because of the many health benefits provided by soy, it's becoming more and more popular in other cultures as well. Soy has a superb protein profile, it's highly palatable, and it offers protective health properties as demonstrated by the populations who consume this superfood. Despite all these reasons, there are people who fear this food too.

Most of the confusion and controversy that surrounds soy is focused on the isoflavones content and how this antioxidant affects the body. In particular, the plant estrogens or phytoestrogens which have a similar chemical structure to our own estrogen hormone. Interestingly enough, these same compounds aren't always mimicking our estrogen. For instance, in specific tissues, these may block the actions of estrogen. This happens when the compounds disrupt the natural estrogens which are far more potent from binding to the estrogen receptors.

Since estrogen plays an important role in the way our bodies function, researchers have tried to study how the phytoestrogen compounds of soy offer similar effects. Although there have been many studies about this, their conclusions don't point to the same thing. While some studies fuel the fear felt about people about soy, other studies claim that there's really nothing to be worried about. In fact, soy is a healthy food which more people should add to their diets.

To help put your mind at ease, let's take a look at the most common concerns people have about soy, which make them reluctant to start eating this superfood:

- **Breast cancer**

  Although the estrogen our bodies naturally produce may promote breast cancer, there's no evidence which suggests that phytoestrogens cause the development of this disease. As a matter of fact, there was one particular study which summed up the evidence about this topic (Hilakivi-Clarke, et al., Is Soy Consumption Good or Bad for the Breast? 2010). The results of this study showed that women who consume soy in moderation actually have a reduced risk of developing breast cancer than women who don't consume the superfood.

- **Menopause**

  For women experiencing menopause, soy may be beneficial to help reduce the common symptoms. But from all the studies which have been conducted about this, there have been conflicting results. Therefore, the efficacy of soy remains unclear.

- **"Man boobs"**

  Obviously, this belief is one of the main reasons

why men don't want to add soy to their diets. But contrary to popular beliefs, men who eat soy aren't likely to develop "man boobs" or other feminine features. If you need more convincing, you may refer to the review performed in 2010 (Messina, Soybean isoflavone exposure does not have feminizing effects on men: a critical examination of the clinical evidence, 2010).

Here, the researchers indicated that there isn't any evidence which shows how exposure to isoflavones can affect circulating estrogen in men. Although men who consume extremely high amounts of this superfood may develop enlarged and tender breast tissue, overall, it's very very rare for average men to experience these effects.

What Does the Research Say About Soy?

It's hard to determine the exact cause of soy's bad reputation. It's one of the many nutrition mysteries that a lot of us have started believing ever since we heard it. But what does science have to say about this issue? Let's take a look at some of the most significant misconceptions about soy along with some studies which prove them wrong:

- **Breast cancer**

A study conducted in 2008 showed the relationship between breast cancer and soy (Wu AH, et al., Epidemiology of soy exposures and breast cancer risk, 2008). The results of this study showed that women who consumed the most soy in different forms had a 29% less likelihood of developing breast cancer compared to women who ate minimal to no amounts of soy.

In another study, researchers also discovered a preventive effect from consuming soy, this time reducing the risk of developing breast cancer by 41% (Chen, et al., Association between soy isoflavone intake and breast cancer risk for pre- and post-menopausal women: a meta-analysis of epidemiological studies, 2014).

In terms of recurrence, a study conducted in 2012 involved survivors of breast cancer (Nechuta, et al., Soy food intake after diagnosis of breast cancer and survival: an in-depth analysis of combined evidence from cohort studies of US and Chinese women, 2012). Through the study, the researchers discovered that women who consumed the most soy had a 30% less likelihood of their cancer recurring compared to women who consumed minimal to no amounts of soy.

- **Male hormones**

There was a meta-analysis conducted on men which showed that consuming soy or taking isoflavone supplements doesn't have an effect on the levels of testosterone in men (Hamilton-Reeves, et al., Clinical studies show no effects of soy protein or isoflavones on reproductive hormones in men: results of a meta-analysis, 2010).

In another study, the researchers discovered that men who consumed more soy showed a 26% reduction in the risk of developing prostate cancer (Yan, et al., Soy consumption and prostate cancer risk in men: a revisit of a meta-analysis, 2009). For those who consumed non-fermented soy products like tofu and soymilk, the reduction of this risk was up to 30%.

- **Thyroid health**

Clinical studies have shown that soy and soy products don't cause hypothyroidism (Messina & Redmond, Effects of soy protein and soybean isoflavones on thyroid function in healthy adults and hypothyroid patients: a review of the relevant literature, 2006). However, the researchers did find out that soy products may reduce the body's ability to absorb medications used for the treatment of hypothyroidism. So, if you're fond of soy, you may want to check with your doctor if you need to make adjustments to your medication dosage.

In an older study, the researchers discovered that the isoflavones content of soy might consume some of the iodine that the body normally uses to produce the thyroid hormone (Divi, et al., Anti-thyroid isoflavones from soybean: isolation, characterization, and mechanisms of action, 1997). However, the same effect is caused by some types of medications and fiber supplements.

Chapter 8: Should You Buy Organic?

If you live in America, chances are, you are very familiar with the term 'organic' and you probably hear about organic foods a lot. More and more shops, grocery stores, and health stores are stacking their shelves with organic produce and other food items to appeal to those who are looking for healthier options. But if you go vegan, does this automatically mean that you should only buy organic?

The simple answer to this question is, no, you don't have to, especially if organic products don't really fit into your budget. The sad thing is that since producers know that consumers seek out organic products, they tend to give these products higher price tags. So, if going vegan means ONLY buying organic products, this becomes yet another reason for people not to make this lifestyle choice.

What Does Organic Mean?

What does organic really mean? What makes these

products more superior than others? According to the USDA, the objective of organic farming and the production of organic foods is the integration of mechanical, biological, and cultural practices that conserve biodiversity, promote the cycling of resources, and foster the balance of the ecology.

This means that if you purchase an item which has a seal indicating that it's "Certified Organic" or "USDA Organic," this means that the contents and ingredients of the product must be at least 95% or more free of chemical fertilizers, dyes, pesticides, and other synthetic additives. Also, products with this seal shouldn't have been processed with irradiation, genetic engineering, or industrial solvents.

Sometimes, you might also see products with a seal that says, "100% Organic." For such products, this means that all of the contents or ingredients must completely comply with all of the requirements above. For those which indicate "Made with Organic," such products must have at least 70% contents or ingredients which are organic.

If a product contains any of these seals, it means that the manufacturer has followed the rules and guidelines of the USDA regarding organic products. Any violations of these rules would subject the company to civil penalties. With so many organic products flooding the markets these days, some people are starting to feel skeptical about the authenticity of the seal and the claims on the product's labels. If you want to make sure that you're getting truly organic products, then you must do your research.

Of course, the best thing to do would be to purchase your organic products from well-known and reputable brands. However, if your budget doesn't allow for such high-priced food items, then you may have to go for products from lesser known brands. After all, it wouldn't be too practical for you to break the bank just to support your vegan lifestyle.

Tips for Buying Produce When You Don't Choose Organic

You can't deny the fact that fruits and vegetables are significantly more affordable than fish, meat, eggs, and dairy products. So, if you cut these out from your shopping list, you may be able to save enough money for organic produce! But if you've already crunched the numbers, canvassed for products in your local grocery stores and farmers markets, and you find out that your budget really doesn't allow you to purchase organic products regularly, that's okay too! Just make sure that you wash the fruits and vegetables thoroughly or soak them in water for around half an hour before eating them raw.

Generally, it's alright for you to purchase regular food items as a vegan. Just because you've started your vegan journey, this doesn't mean that you should only require yourself to purchase organic products in order to "stay healthy." As I've said, if you can't afford it, this just isn't practical.

Take me, for example. Although I do go for organic products once in a while, I don't make these parts of my regular shopping list. If I have the budget for it, then I pick out some fresh, organic produce along with the rest of my items. If not, then I go for the usual products I've purchased since even before I was a vegan. I just make sure to wash and prepare all of these ingredients properly to make sure they are safe and free from impurities.

Another strategy I've discovered is to purchase different kinds of products from different kinds of stores. For instance, if you only purchase all of your vegan meal prep needs at health stores, you might find your food budget dwindling faster than you can keep up. It's not just about what you buy (meaning, organic products); it's also where you buy your stocks. In order to find the best deals, you may want to go around the different shops in your area. Then make a note of the products each of these shops carries which offer the best prices. So, when it's time to restock, then you know exactly where to go!

If you're a fan of meal prepping, you may also want to purchase your food items in bulk as this tends to be cheaper. Just make sure that the food items you buy in bulk aren't perishable. Come up with your meal plans and see which ingredients you use often. For these ingredients, you can purchase more of them at a time, so you don't have to keep restocking often. If you're wondering where you can buy a variety of vegan-friendly food items which are not necessarily organic, try visiting:

- Discount or conventional grocery stores

- Produce or market stands

- Dollar stores

- Bulk stores

- Health food stores

- Your own garden!

Watch out for pesticides!

One of the biggest concerns regarding non-organic produce is the possible pesticide content of fruits and vegetables. A lot of people believe that organic produce is more superior because pesticides aren't used when growing them. Pesticides are harmful substances used on plants to prevent infestation of insects while they're growing. Unfortunately, these pesticides also have harmful effects on our health and on the environment.

If your main reason for choosing organic produce is to avoid pesticides, then you should know the list of the "dirtiest" produce which means that these are the ones which tend to be most laden with pesticides. When choosing organic over regular produce, go for these fruits and vegetables:

- **Apples**

  Apples may contain up to 40 different kinds of pesticides, including neurotoxins, reproductive or developmental toxins, carcinogens, and suspected hormone disruptors. This is because apples are highly susceptible to fungus and insect threats, which is why farmers keep spraying different kinds of chemicals over these fruits.

- **Blueberries**

  This fruit contains more than 50 different types of pesticides. For blueberries, if you can't find organic ones, you may choose the frozen variety which is slightly less contaminated than the fresh ones.

- **Celery**

  For this vegetable, farmers may use up to 60 different kinds of pesticides when growing them. If you're not able to find organic celery in your local shops, you can try using broccoli or onions in your dishes instead.

- **Grapes**

  This fruit contains more than 30 different pesticides, most of which are potential neurotoxins and hormone disruptors. Be wary of imported grapes too as these might even contain higher levels of residue from pesticides compared to the local varieties.

- **Kale**

  Although kale is hailed as one of the modern superfoods, you might only be able to enjoy all the health benefits if you purchase the organic variety. Non-organic kale contains around 55 different kinds of pesticides which don't make it as healthy as everyone says it is!

- **Lettuce**

  This leafy green vegetable contains more than 50 different kinds of pesticides so you may want to rethink adding this to your salad unless it's organic. Otherwise, you may go for cabbage, which is a lot less contaminated than this popular veggie.

- **Nectarines**

  Although this fruit may only contain up to 33 different types of pesticides, that's still a lot compared to other kinds of produce. Of these pesticides, around 7 of them are carcinogens so you may want to opt for the organic version.

- **Peaches**

  This is another type of fruit which may contain up to 60 different kinds of pesticides. Because of the fuzzy skin of the fruit, it becomes vulnerable to molds and insects, which is why farmers spray these chemicals on them. Unfortunately, the fruits tend to retain these pesticides even after harvesting.

- **Spinach**

  For this vegetable, it may contain up to 48 different kinds of pesticides, making it the most pesticide-laden type of leafy green veggie. The most common types of pesticides used on spinach are dimethoate and permethrin, which are potential carcinogens for us humans.

- **Strawberries**

  This fruit may contain up to 60 different kinds of pesticides. Since this fruit doesn't have a hard, protective skin to cover the delicate flesh, these pesticides can easily seep through the flesh.

- **Sweet bell peppers**

  This vegetable contains almost 50 different kinds

of pesticides no matter which color the pepper may be. Popular as this veggie is in cooking, the pesticides include possible carcinogens, neurotoxins, hormone disruptors, and bee toxins.

- **White potatoes**

  This is one of the most commonly used veggies in the world. You'd think they would be spared from pesticides because they grow underground, but you'd be sadly mistaken. Potatoes contain around 37 different types of pesticides, which is why they're on the "dirty" list too.

Chapter 9: Why Don't You Just Eat Humanely Killed, Happy Cows?

Just by reading the question of this chapter, you may have gotten an idea of the next few topics we will be discussing. For a lot of vegans, myself included, we don't just make a choice to go vegan for health reasons. Part of the vegan journey is to learn about the production of animal products, and this is where things can get highly controversial.

Starting with this chapter and the next five chapters, I will be talking about some "tough topics." Even if you're not an animal lover, learning about the lives of the animals bred, raised, and used in farming and food industries may be the last straw which will push you to become a vegan. As early as now, I would like to warn you that I will be talking about slaughter, slaughterhouses, and the often-savage food industry which provides meat eaters with the animal-products they love to eat so much.

These are tough topics which aren't recommended for sensitive people. If you're one such person, you do have the option to skip this chapter all the way to chapter 14.

But if you really want to learn all that you can about veganism, then you may continue. With that being said, let's start with the life of dairy cows.

What Does Humane Mean in This Context?

By definition, humane means showing or having benevolence or compassion. But how can we call ourselves humane when we accept the killing of animals who don't want to die? What's worse, these animals are raised in horrible conditions AND THEN killed to satisfy the cravings of people all over the world.

Can you still call an act humane if it involves killing?

This is a very difficult question to answer, especially when you learn more about how animals are treated in the food industry. This information that I'm sharing isn't meant to make anyone feel bad. I just want to share what I have learned through my own research. Trust me, learning all this from here is a lot easier to stomach than when you try to learn using more graphics sources.

These days a lot of people use "humane slaughter" to make themselves feel better about the animal food industry. In this process, the animals are first "stunned" before having their throats slit. This is said to be a "humane" way to kill the animals since it's quick and it doesn't cause them pain because they are unconscious. Unfortunately, the laws of humane slaughter aren't really strictly enforced.

Also, consumers are becoming more and more aware of the inefficacy of these stunning practices. Therefore, the animals still undergo tremendous suffering and pain. If an animal isn't stunned the first time, they are either electrocuted or shot in the head several times just to render them unconscious. Then if all else fails, their throats are slit anyway even while fully conscious.

Although this doesn't really seem to be humane (because it's really not!), this is how the process of humane slaughter goes. So, let me ask you again, can this act really be called humane?

A Controversial Topic

Humane slaughter isn't the only excuse the animal food industry has under its belt. Sometimes, they argue by saying that they do provide the animals with a good environment and feed them nutritious food to keep them healthy. But again I ask 'Does this give them the right to kill the animals?' That's another highly controversial question for you to think about.

I didn't start my life as a vegan. As a lot of vegans in the world, I was once a meat eater who ate anything and who believed everything my parents told me about health, food, and nutrition. I knew that meat, eggs, and milk came from animals, but that didn't really bother me. But when I learned about the animals' side of this topic, I realized that I didn't want to take part in it at all.

There's no argument about it; factory farming is nothing but cruel. As a matter of fact, even a lot of meat eaters agree that the practices being done here aren't acceptable. They prefer meat which comes from "humane slaughterhouses" and organic farms. But there are no farms anywhere in the world where the animals are allowed to roam freely in green pastures to enjoy their lives. Even if these farms exist, if they are just raised to be killed and eaten, how can we still consider this humane?

The main problem with not accepting the practices of factory farming while you still continue to consume animal products is that this involves selective moral consideration. Think about it, how does a cow being forced to produce milk or killed for beef differ from your pet who you love and cuddle all day? The answer is: they aren't different at all. This is why a lot of people go vegan after learning more about the animal food industry. It's because we decided to pick a side!

The Truth Behind the Myth

The more you learn about these supposedly "happy cows," and all the other animals in the food industry, the more you will change your perspectives and decisions. You can either choose to continue eating animals and animal products while trying to justify this choice with a thousand excuses or you can accept the facts you've learned and made a choice based on those facts.

Have you ever tried to think about why people call them "happy cows?" Generally, when you compare how cows which are raised for beef live compared to cows who are raised for milk, chances are, those raised for beef live a "happier" life. Although the modern-day grass-fed beef cows do experience some good days, they still end up the same way as other animals who live their lives just to be slaughtered and eaten.

When that time comes, these cows are transported to feedlots where they remain there for around 3-4 months eating corn and other grains. This diet allows for faster growth of the cows where their meat is marbled with fat making them perfect for consumption. Sadly, this diet isn't suited for the digestive systems of cows because it leads to chronic GI distress and severe liver problems. Then as soon as the cows are fat enough, they are transported to slaughterhouses where they will meet their fate.

This is the typical life cycle of cows which are raised for beef, even those which are labeled as "humane meat." Although there may be small farms out there where the cows live significantly more comfortable lives for a time, you must also realize that the humane labels you find on expensive cuts of beef are nothing more than a marketing ploy meant to prey on the willingness of consumers to pay a higher price for animals which are "treated better."

But if you really care for these animals and you don't want to contribute to their suffering, what can you do? For a start, you can try to consider veganism. You don't have to do it overnight; it can be a gradual process. You can start by cutting out one type of animal product every month or so until you've finally eliminated all animal foods from your life. Then you can confidently say that you're making a contribution to the downfall of the animal food industry in your own little way. And the best part is, you'll be enjoying a lot of long-term health benefits too!

The Choice is Yours

Before I became vegan, I never even thought about this and about all the other animals being raised for food. Today I think about the animals more and this turned to be my main reason for staying vegan. What do the cows think when they're on their way to the slaughterhouse? They're stuffed into a truck with dozens of other cows who are all feeling frightened.

Then they're lined up and herded to a ramp where they will meet their untimely demise. Although cows may not know what's coming, they definitely feel scared to death. To kill the cows, they get shot with a bolt then are hoisted up by one of their legs. Then their throats are slit, and their skin is peeled off. After this, the bodies of cows are cut up, and finally, wrapped in bags and cradles.

This is a horrible ordeal which those who buy meat don't know or think about. They don't feel the stress, the shock, the fear, and the death of the animals. The pieces of meat are just part of the grocery lists. Now that you know this, the choice is yours. But we're just getting started. This is just about cows raised for beef!

Chapter 10: The Life of a Milk Cow

When you were growing up, did you believe that you needed to drink milk so that you can grow big and strong? If you did, you're not alone.

Do you know how long are human children supposed to drink milk? Generally, children are weaned from milk when they reach the age of three. But for some people, this age may already be too late for their babies to stop drinking milk. So why do we still drink milk as we grow older? And when we're weaned from our mother's milk by 3 years old, why should we continue to drink milk from the mothers of other species like cows, goats, and more?

It's because this is what we have been taught, and this is what we know. That in order to grow big, strong, and to get enough calcium, we should drink milk while we're growing up. But do the cows give their milk willingly? Let's find out.

A Sad and Painful Life

At one point in any female cow's life, she will start giving milk. For the sake of argument, let's assume that this happens because this is the purpose of her life. A lot of us are led to believe that once female cows start producing milk, they produce this liquid in excess. And so, farmers help these female cows to "not explode" by milking them. Then when these female cows stop producing milk because they reach menopause, these farmers thank the cows and send them off to retirement.

There's nothing wrong with this scenario, is there?

Well, the one thing wrong with this scenario is that it just doesn't happen this way. If you feel okay with drinking cow's milk because you think you're doing them a favor, then you might just change your mind when you find out the truth about the sad and painful life of dairy cows. Here is how their lives go:

As an example, let's take the life of a dairy cow named Emily. Most likely, Emily was artificially inseminated so that she can give birth to a calf, and her body can start producing milk for nursing. After giving birth, Emily feels happy and proud of her bundle of joy. Unfortunately, these positive feelings won't last long because humans need Emily's milk. So, the farmers take her calf away from her.

As her baby is taken from her, both Emily and her calf are devastated and traumatized.

They cry for weeks. Now Emily is a milk cow. She is milked twice a day for the next 9-10 months. When Emily's milk production declines, she will get a 2-3-monht 'rest'. After she has rested and her udders have healed from the 10-month milking period, she will be re-impregnated. She would to go through this traumatic cycle of shock and pain every time she is separated from her calf. Like Emily, every milk cow can only go through three to five cycles of pregnancies before they are no longer usable as milk cows. When Emily can no longer give milk, this will be time to slather her.

So, this wasn't a happy-ending story but unfortunately this is the reality. And I've never thought about this scenario when I used to buy milk. I know that many people don't either. I also know that it takes time for people to open their minds and see with their hearts. A friend of mine for example, not long time ago said that all this 'cows-have-miserable-life' talk is BS. This was simply because he has seen 5-6 cows gazing grass in the nature and because he 'thought' that cows give milk all-year-around with no need to give birth whatsoever.

And don't get me wrong – not only don't I blame him, but I absolutely get him. That used to be me. I used to think that dairy cows look the way we see them on the milk cartons – having lots of joy in green pastures, together with their calves, not-minding being milked occasionally, living long and happy life.

What I think now is that dairy cows have a life filled with stress, anxiety, and vanity. All they've got is a pitiable existence which ends with an untimely death.

This is the life of all dairy cows, not just Emily. They never get to raise their children, they never grow old, and they never get to enjoy their lives.

Imagine living such a life. Imagine if you lived all your life in a single farmhouse where you had to undergo pregnancies over and over again just for farmers to take your children away from you because the milk you produce for them will be given to other animals.

The worst part is, the process doesn't even end there. Have you ever wondered what happens to the calves after being taken away from their mothers? For female calves, they are given formula milk until they're old enough to become dairy cows themselves. After a couple of months, they are then impregnated so they can undergo the same process their mothers experienced before them.

For male calves, the farmers will first determine the state of the baby bull. Some of them may be raised to sire cattle, others are sent to veal farms where they are kept in crates for about 18 months then slaughtered, and the "lucky ones" are sent to "humane" veal farms where they are allowed to run around and eat grass for the same amount of time (18 months) before they're slaughtered and packaged as "rose veal." Now that you know all of this, has it changed how you perceive cow's milk and other types of dairy products?

From Dairy and Milk Farmers to Vegan Activists

After learning the truth about dairy cows, you may start re-considering your choice to drink a lot of milk and other dairy products. Again, you're not the only one. For a lot of vegans, their decision to go vegan was significantly influenced by the knowledge of how animals are being treated in the food industry.

In fact, there are a lot of dairy and milk farmers all over the world who have become vegan activists fighting for those they used to oppress. Here are some of the most notable ones who prove that there is hope for ANYONE to change:

- **Jan Gerdes**

  Jan used to be a dairy farmer in Germany for several years. But since going vegan, he converted his farm into a sanctuary for cows. He has then devoted his life to really caring for farm animals and working hard to end animal exploitation.

- **Chris Mills**

  Chris worked in Ontario for over 20 years on dairy farms before he decided to become a vegan. Although he was an avid hunter and trapper, he ended up with a vegetarian wife. Now Chris and his wife transformed their small property into "The Grass Is Greener Farm Sanctuary."

- **Harold Brown**

  Harold used to be a farmer of both beef and dairy cows. He was born into a family of cow farmers, and so he grew up knowing all about this business. But when he experienced a health crisis because heart disease runs in his family, he decided to become a vegan. Now, Harold is a vegan activist; he founded "Farm Kind," and he was one of the subjects of a documentary entitled "The Peaceable Kingdom."

- **Cheri Ezell**

  Although Cheri and her husband used to work in the dairy industry, they had left and even converted their farm into a safe place for wildlife, companion animals, and farmed animals. Here, they practice true humane farming where the animals under their care aren't killed for meat. Instead, the couple cultivates a plant-based diet.

- **Susana Romatz**

  Finally, Susana used to be a goat dairy farmer. But when she was old enough to understand the implications and effects of dairy farming on animals, she decided to make a change. She is now an avid mushroom forager, and she now works in a hazelnut milking industry. She is also a vegan activist who isn't afraid to speak out about how animal treatment in the food industry must come to an end.

Seeing people like these make a huge transition gives hope to those who are thinking of going vegan but aren't sure if they can do it. But if these ethical reasons aren't enough, maybe the health reasons can help convince you better.

Is Milk from Cows Even Healthy?

If you grew up drinking cow's milk and you love the stuff, I don't blame you for not wanting to give up just like that. But apart from the ethical reasons for eliminating animal milk from your diet, maybe these health reasons can convince you.

There are several studies which have shown that whether

you're lactose intolerant or not, consuming dairy every day tends to increase the IGF-1 hormone. Milk from cows contains testosterone, estradiol, and other steroid hormones along with peptide hormones like IGF-1. Although this hormone does have benefits to the body, high levels in the body may increase the risk of developing certain types of cancer.

Of course, this isn't the only reason why cow's milk isn't actually good for us. Here are some other reasons for you to consider:

- **It's not really good for your bones**

  I've mentioned how a lot of us grew up believing that we should drink milk in order to grow big and strong. Part of this spiel was how cow's milk was rich in calcium, thus, making it good for the bones. Although cow's milk does contain calcium, it's also important to note that when our bodies break animal proteins down, this produces acid.

  For our bodies to neutralize this acid and flush it out, it uses calcium. If you consume a lot of acidic foods and you drink a lot of cow's milk too, your body will use up the calcium content of the milk along with some of the stored calcium in the body. Therefore, when you drink a lot of cow's milk and other animal-based dairy products, this ends up leaching the calcium from your bones.

- **It may cause prostate cancer**

  Milk, cheese, and other dairy products have been associated with an increased risk of developing prostate cancer. As for diets which are free of dairy, these may slow the progress of this type of cancer.

- **It's not good for those who are lactose intolerant**

  For some people, cow's milk is difficult to digest. This is why some people experience lactose intolerance because their bodies cannot handle cow's milk properly. In such cases, you may experience diarrhea, bloating, cramps, gas, and nausea. And if you keep on drinking cow's milk, this may cause your symptoms to worsen progressively.

- **It can cause acne**

  Several studies have shown that consuming cow's milk and all other kinds of animal-derived dairy products can increase your prevalence of acne. In some cases, this may also increase the severity of existing acne in both genders. An amazing example of curing acne by going vegan is Youtuber Cassandra Bankson. She documented her battle fighting acne and how adopting plant-based diet made the biggest difference for her skin health.

- **It may elevate the levels of cholesterol**

  One serving of milk may contain as much as 24 mg of cholesterol, which is harmful to the heart. So, the more you drink cow's milk and products which contain cow's milk, the more this might elevate your cholesterol levels.

- **It may cause ovarian cancer**

  There was a study conducted in Sweden about this (Larsson, et al., Milk and lactose intakes and ovarian cancer risk in the Swedish Mammography Cohort, 2004). The results of the study showed that women who consumed four or more servings of cow's milk and other dairy products were twice as likely to develop ovarian cancer compared to those who consumed minimal to no amounts of dairy.

- **Some people are allergic to cow's milk**

  Although this doesn't apply to everyone, there are some people who experience allergic reactions after drinking cow's milk. Such reactions can be very dangerous, especially in the case of anaphylaxis.

- **Dairy cows are often injected with antibiotics**

In order to keep dairy cows alive and to continue their milk production, farmers pump them full of antibiotics. Farmers overuse these antibiotics because of the surge in bacteria which are resistant to them. When you get infected by these bacteria, the antibiotics you take might not be as effective to treat your infection.

- **Cow's milk contains a lot of saturated fat**

One serving of whole cow's milk contains over 20% of your recommended daily allowance of saturated fat. So, if you consume more, you will also be consuming high levels of saturated fat even before you eat anything.

- **It may cause weight gain**

With all that saturated fat and other unnecessary compounds, drinking too much cow's milk can cause weight gain in people of all ages. If one of your goals is to lose weight, you may want to stay away from this particular drink and all other products which contain it.

The Dangers of Milk Production

The biggest danger of milk production is the growth hormones given to cows. These promote the growth of the dairy cows while helping increase their milk production too. Although the use of these growth hormones is illegal in some countries, there are unscrupulous farmers who have no problem breaking the law.

Just as with people, everything that goes into the bodies of cows will end up affecting their health in one way or another. The diet of modern cows includes straw, roots, grass, legumes, silage, oilcakes, tubers, cereals, and even milk by-products which contain different chemical additives. Dairy cows have diets which are full of herbicides, fertilizers, pesticides, and even some traces of chemicals from spoilage and heavy metals too. Therefore, when you consume cow's milk and other dairy products continuously, this puts you at risk for a host of diseases and illnesses such as infections, atherosclerosis, some types of cancer, and more.

Also, when you continue drinking cow's milk, you will also consume high amounts of IGF-1, the peptide hormone which I have mentioned in the previous section. This hormone is a key factor in the growth and development of lung, prostate, and breast cancer. It's a powerful hormone because it stimulates the growth of all cells, not just healthy ones. So, when IGF-1 interacts with cancer cells, it sends a message for them to keep growing (Cohen, Milk – The Deadly Poison, 1998)!

Chapter 11: What About Eggs?

What about eggs? Is it okay to eat these? If you plan to start your vegan journey by becoming a vegetarian first, it would be best if you only get your eggs from a farmer whom you personally know.

But what's wrong with eggs? There are vegans who eat eggs on occasion and aren't dropping dead from heart attacks. Yes, eggs are rich in protein, minerals and vitamins. What else they are rich in is cholesterol.

If your reasons for becoming a vegan are ethical, then you probably won't eat eggs after you find out the truth about egg farms.

However, if you're more focused on your health and you really believe that you can still be healthy when eating eggs once in a while, that decision lies with you. Remember, the vegan journey is all about your own pace. If you try to restrict yourself too much, this might be counterproductive to your goal.

How Do the Chickens Live Their Lives?

Much as I'd like to tell you that chickens have it easier so you can continue eating eggs even if you have ethical reasons for becoming vegan, this just isn't true. Remember how I mentioned that these chapters are the tough ones, so let's continue with the truth about how those eggs end up on the shelves.

Most egg-laying chickens are imprisoned in cages where there would be around 5, 6 or even more chickens in each cage. You may think, "well, that's not too bad." But the thing is, these cages are often too small for even a single hen to spread one of her wings! So, most of these chickens live their whole lives without space, without ever seeing the light of day, ill, and only laying eggs in the same place where they defecate.

Chickens are actually intelligent and social creatures. They like communicating with each other socially, and they tend to establish status within their flocks. These are the natural instincts of chickens which they never get to experience when they are born and raised in farming environments. Since the chickens are kept in small, confined spaces, they end up becoming aggressive towards each other.

To help prevent the chickens from tearing each other apart, the farming industry came up with what they believe is an "innovative method" known as debeaking. In reality, this is an extremely painful procedure where the beaks of the hens are either cut or burned away until almost nothing is left. If you weren't aware, the beak of a chicken is the most sensitive tissue they possess.

So aside from living in horrible conditions, the chickens also have no choice but to undergo debeaking. All of this causes high stress, which, in turn, causes the chickens to develop psychoses. As they're forced to lay eggs, their muscles start to atrophy, and their bones start to soften. You can only imagine how miserable the lives of these hens are.

But what of the male chickens? Since they don't lay eggs, farmers don't see the need to feed and raise them. So, you won't see a lot of male chickens in such farms. The hens are artificially inseminated for them to keep on laying eggs. Either that or the farmers maintain one rooster to inseminate the entire flock. Therefore, when the chicks that hatch from eggs are male, most of them are just killed shortly after they hatch. This is done by tossing the live chicks into a piece of equipment known as a macerator, the same machine which is used to grind solid waste. So, let me ask you this: what part of all this is humane?

What About Free-Range Eggs?

Let me tell you something: I LOVED eggs! I loved them for the taste, for their versatility and for their protein content. I used to have eggs every single day! Since I was and still am actively practicing sports, eggs were my favorite breakfast, lunch or afternoon snack.

What happened? Well, I saw some of the horrifying videos that I've been avoiding watching for a very long time. It happened that I passed by some Vegan Activists on the street. They all had 'anonymous' masks on and were holding screens showing footages from factory farms and slaughterhouses. I saw them and slowed down only because of curiosity. I had no idea why they were standing there. A lady approached me and explained that they are spreading the word and having conversations with people about the harm of the meat industry. Honestly, I wasn't really opened to accept what she was saying to me, but I glanced the screens those people were holding. I watched for a couple of minutes. I was frozen. I saw that, from birth to death, these poor animals are caught in a nightmare: cruelly confined, brutally mutilated, and sadistically killed. So, the seed was planted, as they say.

The common belief is that free-range hens live their lives freely being able to run around pecking at insects, grass, and anything else they find on the ground. Then they lay eggs here and there without having to suffer. This belief allowed me to enjoy eggs without feeling guilty.

Although it's true that free-range hens don't live in conditions as dismal as those at factory farms, the way they live their lives is still a far cry from how they should naturally live if they were left alone. In fact, the methods practiced by farmers in free-range facilities are a lot like the ones practiced by those in factory farms. They still keep the chickens in cages albeit with more space and the chickens also undergo debeaking. Also, when the hens are no longer able to lay eggs, they are slaughtered just like the ones in factory farms.

But what is wrong with eggs themselves? - you might ask. There are vegans who occasionally have eggs, or a bit of cheese, or yoghurt and they are not dropping dead from heart attacks.

You can look up and find studies that research and advocate both points - that eggs are healthy and unhealthy. If you find a study that concludes eggs are good for you and it resonates with you, remember it is your journey, in your pace.

After reading a ton of studies and researches, here is what I found about the health risk associated with eating eggs. Eggs contain cholesterol and saturated fat, both of which are unhealthy for your heart. There have been various works linked to research which revealed that those who consume up to two eggs daily are more likely to develop type-2 diabetes mellitus. In addition, eggs have been implicated to cause hormone-sensitive cancers as well as food poisoning.

Are There Vegan Alternatives to Eggs?

There are many alternatives to eggs, it all depends on what you're trying to make.

Egg replacement for cakes: Unsweetened applesauce or banana may be used as replacements for eggs in pancakes or desserts. I use ½ cup of unsweetened applesauce or one ripe mashed banana. Any of these is equivalent to one egg.

Egg replacement for Yorkshire puddings (meringue): If you wish to make a Yorkshire pudding, chickpea juice or Aquafina is exactly what you need to play the role of an egg in your recipe. You can pour some from the can into a bowl and then whisk it with an electric mixer to make it thicker. Three to four tablespoons of aquafaba will play the role of one full egg.

Other vegan replacements for egg: Chia seed or flaxseed can also be used as replacements for eggs and apart from this, they also have the additional benefit of being tasteless which is something you can't get from an egg. I mix 1 tablespoon of crushed chia or flaxseed with 3 tablespoons of water and let it stay for 5 minutes.

Chapter 12: Poultry Problems

As I've said, chickens are highly social and intelligent creatures. They're able to recognize the members of their flock, and they're also able to recognize human beings. If you assign a name to a chicken, they can even respond to this name. Some people try to avoid pork and meat only choosing to eat chicken and other poultry because they believe that these birds are the "healthier option." However, poultry isn't as healthy as most people believe.

Also, the poultry industry has a devastating effect on the environment. So many birds are slaughtered that this causes water, land, and air pollution because of the deceased carcasses, heavy metals, bacteria, parasites, viruses, feces, chemicals, and pathogen cysts. Poultry slaughterhouses produce huge amounts of waste which poses threats to the environment and to us, humans, too.

Finally, chickens and other types of poultry raised in the food industry receive the same treatment and suffering as cows, pigs, and all other animals. To give you a clearer picture, let's discuss this further.

The Horrible Truth About Poultry Farms

Just like the egg-laying chickens, those chickens who are raised for their meat live their lives in huge warehouses which are extremely crowded. These days, the chickens are genetically manipulated so that they grow bigger and faster than what happens in nature. The upper bodies of these chickens grow at such a high rate that their legs start collapsing. It is notoriously disturbing that these chicks are just 6-week-old. Under normal circumstances, at this age, they would still be sheltered under the wings of their mothers.

Even if some chickens are lucky enough to survive this ordeal, they just end up being slaughtered along with all the other chickens. In these farms, the chickens undergo an extremely painful procedure known as an "electric bath." Here, a painful electric shock immobilizes the birds, but they're still able to feel all the pain. Then all the chickens are gathered together while they are completely aware and alive.

Chickens are the most killed and the most abused animals on the planet. In fact, more chickens are killed all over the world every year than all the other types of land animals put together! Chickens who live in poultry farms aren't able to get the proper nutrition and social interactions which they need to grow into happy and healthy birds. Instead, they're kept in cruel conditions, and after some time, they are slaughtered, in my opinion, in an inhuman way. As these chickens grow in close proximity to each other, a lot of them get sick.

Then when it's time for the chickens to be slaughtered

after their electric bath, their throats are cut, those who survive are scalded until they die, then all their feathers are plucked before their carcasses are packed and shipped to different establishments. What a life!

Why Poultry is Unhealthy

All this suffering and only to find out that poultry isn't actually as healthy as people believe. For one, chicken meat is commonly associated with bacteria such as listeria, campylobacter, and salmonella. Also, the chickens which are bred and raised now are a lot higher in fat compared to the chickens' people ate around 50 years ago. Here are some other reasons I've found that prove that poultry isn't actually healthy:

- Broiler chickens may contain E-coli and other antibiotic-resistant bacteria which may cause UTI and diarrhea.

- Even if you eat chicken sans the skin, it still has a high cholesterol content. When it comes to cholesterol levels, chicken and beef sirloin have nearly the same level.

- Grilling chicken or deep frying it may help increase the risk of developing cancer.

- More and more manufacturers of chicken feed are starting to use arsenic in order to improve pigmentation, prevent diarrhea, and ensure good growth. Unfortunately, arsenic is harmful to humans as it may increase the risk of neurological problems, diabetes, heart disease, and even some forms of cancer.

Although chicken may contain some good nutrients, when you combine the health reasons with the ethical reasons not to eat chicken, it's easier to understand why us vegans have sworn off poultry.

Chapter 13: Pigs Don't Have It Easy Either

I grew up in the countryside. I spent every summer at my grandparents' home who were raising pigs (and not only) for meat. I've seen my grandfather killing them for food and I've never been stroked by the thought that they are living creatures who probably don't want to die. And here is the moment to acknowledge that there are farmers and families breeding animals who truly love them and take good care of them, and so did my grandparents did. They let them out, give them names and pet them and yet, the animals still die.

Pigs are highly intelligent creatures too. In fact, they're the most intelligent animals after dolphins, chimps, and, of course, humans. Aside from their intellect, pigs are also sentient creatures, which means that they experience fear, frustration, loneliness, joy, and pain. Although they share a lot of similarities with dogs, cats, and other pet animals, most of them live their lives in factory farms where all they know is cruelty.

You may have seen a lot of movies and stories about pigs being kept as pets. Good for them! But the majority of these animals aren't so lucky. From the time they are born to the time when they are slaughtered, they live their lives in fear, desperation, pain, and suffering.

The Inescapable Fate of Pigs

Most pigs in factory farms live their lives fearing humans and fearing their inescapable fate: death. Pregnant female pigs are placed in crates while they await the time when they have to give birth. These crates as so small that they aren't even able to move. When these mothers give birth to their piglets, they are kept in a lying position for the purpose of nursing their newborn piglets.

Unfortunately, nursing and living their lives in this one position doesn't make it possible for the mother pigs to stand up or even roll over. This presents a problem because the mother pigs aren't able to get to know their babies; neither are they able to teach their little ones how to behave properly.

After less than one month of nursing from their mothers, the piglets are taken away. Under normal conditions, mother pigs would nurse their piglets for a couple of months. But for those who live in factory farms, they are impregnated over and over again. These female pigs undergo this painful process as many times as their health allows. The mother pigs aren't able to see their piglets grow. And the more times they experience this process, the more these mother pigs become aware of what comes next. It's a sad and cruel cycle which they have no choice but to endure.

If this wasn't bad enough, the piglets suffer as well. Their tails are docked, their ears are notched, the testicles of the male pigs are ripped out, and more, all without any relief from pain. Some piglets get their teeth clipped, which is an act the pig industry justifies as a means of preventing the piglets from causing harm to each other. The truth is pigs barely harm each other even when they live in the wild. The stressful living conditions and overcrowding which these piglets are subjected to is the cause of such violent acts.

And then there are the "eaters." These are the pigs which are bred and fed for their meat. These pigs grow up in cramped environments where all they do is eat food which, for us humans, is repulsive. Often, they are even fed animal by-products which aren't suitable for human consumption. Basically, they live their short lives consuming garbage, vitamin supplements, antibiotics, and chemicals, all of which keep them alive until it's time for them to be slaughtered.

As soon as the pigs are fat enough, they are sent to the slaughterhouse. This usually happens after 6 months or so of continuous eating. Toddler pigs which are sent to the slaughterhouse are stunned then killed by scalding, knife

102

or gas chamber. The first option is the worst because most of the pigs are alive when they're thrown into the hot water baths which remove their hair and make their skin softer. Unfortunately, the process forces them to die excruciating and miserable deaths.

Even during transit, pigs still suffer. When they're transported during the winter months, some of the pigs literally freeze to death, especially if they're pressed against the metal walls of the transport containers. After freezing to death, they even get stuck to the metal. During the summer months, the heat is unbearable when the pigs are transported. Often, they would perish because of heat exhaustion even before they arrive at the slaughterhouse. For those who are still alive, they meet their demise in different ways.

Even the free-range pigs can't escape a life of suffering. The only difference between these pigs and the ones grown in factory farms is that the free-range pigs are given access to the outside world. They're able to walk around, but at the end of the day, they fate is to be sent to slaughterhouses for their meat.

Pork Isn't Even Good for You

Bacon, pork chops, BBQ ribs, and more. There are so

many kinds of dishes centered around pork and meat-eaters love them! Apart from being the most widely eaten meat in the world, pork may also be a reservoir for some of the most dangerous pathogens as well as some underlying health risks. Here are some of the risks you must know about:

- **Hepatitis E**

  In developed countries, pork liver is one of the most common hepatitis E transmitters. This is a type of virus that has infected over 20 million people every year. This virus may lead to fatigue, vomiting, fever, stomach pain, joint pain, jaundice, and other acute illnesses. It may also lead to an enlargement to the liver and, in the more severe cases, liver failure. Hepatitis E is a dangerous disease because it's stealthy and symptom-free. But it's especially dangerous for pregnant women and people with weakened immune systems.

- **Multiple Sclerosis**

  This is one risk associated with eating pork that comes as a surprise to a lot of people. However, people have already been aware of the link between MS and pork since the 1980s. This information first came out when researchers studied the relationship between the occurrence of MS in different countries and the per capita consumption of pork (Nanji & Narod, Multiple sclerosis, latitude, and dietary fat: is pork the missing link? 1986).

- **Cirrhosis and Liver Cancer**

  For years, the consumption of pork has been causing cirrhosis and liver cancer rates to rise all over the world. There have even been studies which focused on this fact. In one specific study, they directly examined the relationship between pork consumption and the development of cirrhosis (Nanji & French, Relationship between pork consumption and cirrhosis., 1985). Here, they discovered a significant correlation between the two, which means that pork consumption may definitely increase the risk of the development of this condition.

- **Yersiniosis**

  This condition is caused by a kind of bacteria known as Yersinia, which is found in undercooked pork. The symptoms of this condition are rough as these include pain, fever, bloody diarrhea, and more. However, the long-term consequences are much more dangerous as this condition may cause reactive arthritis, an inflammatory disease of the joints that is caused by infection. Sadly, this condition can also affect children where they would require an osmic acid injection through a procedure known as synovectomy in order to give them relief from persistent pain.

These are some of the scariest risks that come with pork consumption. Of course, there are other risks such as high cholesterol, high blood, and more. With all these reasons as well as the truth behind the lives of factory farm pigs, you can now understand why we vegans have chosen to eliminate this food from our diets.

Chapter 14: All About Fish

A lot of people believe that fish is a must in our diet. Also, many people believe that the creatures which live underwater have "fish brains" and thus aren't intelligent. But as it turns out, this isn't true at all. In fact, fish possess long-term memory, they have the ability to recognize, and they even have "opinions" about each other!

Although fish differ from us, they also have a consciousness, and they also feel pain. Of course, since we are led to believe that fish is good for our health, a lot of people disagree with these facts. But this is just another way of justifying the killing of fish and other seafood.

Even though fish is "good for the health," as a lot of people say, I have my reasons for eliminating these foods and all the other types of animals from my diet. "But what's wrong with eating fish?" you may ask. Let's take a look at the truth behind the fish and seafood industry.

The Trouble with Farm-Raised Fish

Just like the other animals which live in factory farms, farm-raised fish typically spend their whole lives in crowded environments which are full of their own excrements. These fish have no choice but to suffer from injuries and stress brought about by such living conditions. A lot of fish end up dying because of this. But for those "lucky enough" to survive, they are sent to a "kill plant" where they're poured into huge mesh tanks where they end up suffocating to death.

Diseases are very rampant among farm-raised fish. So, in order to prevent these diseases from spreading and lowering their profits, fish farmers depend on vaccines and other types of medications which stay in the bodies of these fish until humans eat them. This means that whenever you eat farm-raised fish, there's a high likelihood that you're also eating carcinogens such as toxaphene, dieldrin, dioxin, and more.

Because of this, some people opt for wild-caught fish such as salmon. Although you may not be consuming the carcinogens which are present in farm-raised fish, there is a high likelihood that you will be consuming arsenic and mercury. When your blood contains high levels of mercury, this can cause health problems. This is especially harmful to pregnant women because it might cause disabilities or birth defects in the developing fetus.

If this isn't enough, here are a few more issues associated with farm-raised fish you may want to know about:

- **There are several types of farm-raised fish**

which are fed other kinds of fish

This means that fish farmers end up fishing for these "prey fish" such as herring and anchovies just to feed the fish farms all around the world. Since this is an unnatural process, other species which rely on these fish for food such as dolphins, whales, sea lions, and the like end up going hungry or having to fight each other for whatever's left behind. This is one of the many examples of us humans destroying the eco-system.

- **Farm-raised fish experience a lot of stress and pain**

I know I mentioned this already, but it's worth mentioning again to emphasize this fact. There was one study conducted on fish which are injected with bee venom (Sneddon, et al., Do Fish have Nociceptors? Evidence for the Evolution of a Vertebrate Sensory System, 2003). In the study, the researchers discovered the effects of this process, which are a reduction in swimming activity, an increase in breathing rates, and the fish also waited a long time before they started eating. The fish also displayed a rocking behavior which is associated with pain.

Throughout their lives, farm-raised fish live in confined spaces, and when it's time to kill them, this is done through excruciatingly slow and painful ways such as asphyxiation, starvation, and evisceration.

- **The diseases which plague farmed fish are starting to spread to the populations of wild fish**

Again, because of the hyper-confinement of fish in fish farms, this gives rise to parasites and diseases. Unfortunately, these tend to migrate off the fish farms, and when this happens, they start infecting wild fish populations. And since other species depend on these wild fish for their food, they end up getting infected too!

- **The toxins in fish farms are bad for the natural ecosystems**

Since the parasites and diseases which plague the farm-raised fish aren't good for the economy of fish farms, the farmers try to ease the situation by adding chemicals such as antibiotics directly into the water. Obviously, these chemicals seep into the natural ecosystems, which causes immeasurable harm.

- **Farmed fish are so miserable that they're constantly trying to escape**

Considering the living conditions of these fish, who

can blame them? But when these farm-raised fish are able to escape, they start breeding with wild fish. This ends up compromising the gene pool which, in turn, harms the wild fish population.

The Truth About the Health Benefits of Fish

For most people, the only reason they eat fish is that they believe they come with a lot of health benefits. Some of the more common "health benefits" include weight loss, lowering of cholesterol levels, memory improvement, and more. Because of all these advertised health benefits, the demand for fish and seafood grows exponentially.

I am sure you've been informed severally about the important role of omega-3 in your body and that you can only get it by eating fish. We know that our bodies need this nutrient and we have been led to believe that the best way to get it is by eating fish. The truth is that we are never short of omega-3; rather we consume omega-6 excessively.

Omega-3 and omega-6 are also known as polyunsaturated fats since they possess several double bonds. Since our bodies don't produce these fats naturally, we must acquire them from the food we eat. If you don't get enough of these amino acids, you may develop a deficiency and get sick. This is why they're also called "essential fatty acids."

Omega-3s and omega-6s have varied effects as well. While omega-3s are anti-inflammatory, omega-6s actually promote inflammation! Therefore, we should not be consuming excessive amounts of it at all.

Anthropology reports have shown that early humans consumed a ratio of around 2:1, but today that consumption is around 20:1. The extra omega 6 comes from consuming a high amount of processed foods as well as polyunsaturated oils used in cooking which is both rich in omega 6 fatty acids. This is not to say that omega 6 fatty acids are not essential for a healthy living however, but an excessive amount of it in the body can cause an excessive inflammatory response.

Getting the Same Nutrients from Plant-Based Sources

Now that you know the truth behind the fish industry, you may want to consider finding healthier food sources that will provide you with the same nutrients and health benefits. The good news is, plant-based sources can help you with this! Since the most significant nutrient people are looking for when they eat fish is omega-3, here are some suggestions of plant-based food sources you can consume as a replacement for fish:

- **Algal oil**

  This is a type of oil that's derived from algae, and it's also a great source of DHA and EPA. This oil can help improve your memory as well as your overall health. You can mix this in smoothies or take it as a nutritional supplement.

- **Brussels sprouts**

  This cruciferous vegetable contains fiber, vitamin C, vitamin K, and omega-3 fatty acids too. In fact, Brussels sprouts are so rich in these essential fatty acids and other nutrients that they can provide a number of health benefits such as reducing the risk of developing heart disease.

- **Chia seeds**

  This is a superfood which offers a ton of health benefits. Aside from protein and fiber, chia seeds are also an excellent source of ALA omega-3 fatty acids. When you consume these seeds as part of your healthy vegan diet, this can help reduce the risk of developing chronic diseases too.

- **Flax seeds**

113

These seeds are considered a nutritional powerhouse as they contain good amounts of protein, fiber, manganese, magnesium, and, of course, omega 3. They can help lower bad cholesterol levels, blood pressure, and they're easy to incorporate in any kind of diet.

- **Hemp seed**

  Another great plant-based source of omega-3 fatty acids, hemp seeds are also rich in zinc, iron, magnesium, and protein. Some health benefits of these seeds include aiding in heart attack recovery, preventing the formation of blood clots, and more.

- **Perilla oil**

  This oil is derived from perilla seeds, and it's a flavorful ingredient to different dishes. It's rich in omega-3 fatty acids, and it helps combat damage caused by free radicals.

- **Walnuts**

  These nuts are packed with ALA omega-3 fatty acids and other healthy fats. They can help improve the health of your brain, reduce anxiety, develop motor skills, and more.

Chapter 15: Does Going Vegan Mean Giving Up Hotdogs, Pizza, Burgers, and More?

Going vegan doesn't mean that you're sacrificing your life for the sake of your ethics or your health. It also doesn't mean that you'll be eating plain old salads for the rest of your life. What kind of life would that be, right?

Even if you go vegan, you can still eat those "cheat day" foods such as hotdogs, pizza, burgers, and so on. It's just that when you're vegan, these would mean different kinds of foods, not the usual fare you would see in fast food chains, street vendor stalls, and more.

Surprisingly to many of my friends, I enjoy large yummy burgers on average once every two weeks. Fortunately, burgers can be made from literally anything. They can be made from veggies, chickpeas, lentils, beans, soy, quinoa, sweet potatoes and so much more.

And trust me, there are so many great options out there that you'll forget why you were worried about this diet change in the first place!

Give Mock Meat a Try

Nowadays, there are so many different types of mock meat products available. From tofu hot dogs to fake chicken nuggets, ground "beef," veggie burgers, and more, there are so many choices for you! Although one of the main goals of going vegan is to eat healthier foods, you can give these mock meat products a try if you're craving for meat:

- **Deli "meat"**

  There are different types of sliced deli mock meats available for those who used to love sliced deli meats. Vegan-friendly mock deli meats are free of MSG, nitrites, cholesterol, and fat. However, they do contain a lot of sodium and oftentimes gluten, so you shouldn't eat a lot of these deli slices if you want to stay healthy.

- **Chick-un nuggets and patties**

  Who doesn't love chicken nuggets? These are so popular that they're almost a staple. There are so many types of chick-un nugget and patty products available out there, and you may opt for these if you're feeling particularly hungry for chicken. That way, you can stick to your diet while still enjoying some tasty nuggets and patties. Of course, just like their real chicken counterparts, remember that these are highly processed products too. So, you may want to avoid eating too many of these.

- **Veggie hotdogs**

  There's no need for you to feel left out when you have a family cookout which involves hotdogs and other scrumptious snacks. Veggie dogs and veggie sausages are available, and they contain more protein, less sodium, less fat, and fewer calories than the regular hot dogs. However, the downside of these veggie versions is they contain an ingredient which holds the "meat" together, and this is called vegetable gum carrageenan. So maybe it's best just to enjoy these on special occasions.

- **Ground "beef"**

  You can find ground mock beef products in supermarkets. They have a similar texture to ground beef, and they usually come blended with seasonings and spices. Conversely, you can also make your own ground "beef" using vegan-friendly ingredients.

- **Veggie burgers**

  Finally, you can also go for veggie burger patties. These are ready to cook, making them highly convenient. Also, there are a lot of varieties out there. Some of them have a fine texture while others are grainier in flavor and they have veggie chunks. You may want to try a few products out to see which ones you prefer the most.

Although there are a lot of choices available, this doesn't mean that you should consume these mock meats at every meal. Yes, they're healthier than real meat (and more ethical too!), but most of these products are still processed. You may consume mock meats occasionally to help you transition into veganism more easily.

Also, remember that not all mock meats are created equal. There are some products which are healthier than others. You should still check the labels of these mock meats to make sure that you're able to choose the healthiest choices. Ultimately, your goal should be to eat as little mock meats and dairy alternatives as possible. They can help satisfy your cravings, but you shouldn't make them the main source of your nutrition. Instead, you should opt for whole foods or dishes which you've cooked yourself for your daily meals.

Why Go Vegan if You'll Eat Mock Meat Anyway? - How to Answer This Question

Mock meats are a normal part of the vegan journey. At one point or another, you may want to try these products, especially when you want to have a taste of meat without guilt or health risks. But when you tell people that you eat mock meats once in a while, they will definitely ask you something like " Why go vegan if you'll eat mock meat anyway?"

When someone asks you this question or something like this, don't take it personally. When you think about it, this is actually a valid question. They just want to know why you gave up meat when you obviously enjoy its taste. Of course, the answer to this question depends on your own reason for becoming a vegan.

For most vegans, I included, we chose to give meat up not because we don't like how it tastes. Rather, eating meat no longer aligned with our ethics and values. Personally, another reason why I gave meat up is that I found out that I can actually get all the nutrients I need from plant-based sources which are, in fact, much healthier.

When you encounter this question, the last thing you want to do is get defensive. Don't start a tirade about how eating meat is unhealthy, wrong, and gross. You might end up offending someone by doing this. If you think it will help, you can try to formulate an answer to this question beforehand. In fact, you can do this right now!

The bottom line is this: If you're asked something about

your lifestyle choice, just answer as honestly and compassionately as possible.

Chapter 16: Taking Baby Steps Towards Veganism

You've made it through the tough chapters! Good for you! If you skipped those chapters, for now, that's okay too. You can go back to them when you're feeling more ready to start learning the truth behind the food industries which turn animals into food. So, what's next?

If you're feeling partially convinced or you're already leaning towards becoming a vegan, then it's time for you to create your action plan. Each vegan journey is different. For me, it took me a while to adjust since I was a voracious meat-eater in the past. I ate a good amount of mock meats to get me through, and I did have to face a few challenges along the way.

For other people, veganism is an easy process. They just make the decision and start with their new lifestyle the very next day. If you're one such person, good for you! But if you're like me, you may have to take "baby steps" towards veganism. To help you out, here are some actionable steps you can start off with. By experience, these are very easy to customize, and these can help make your vegan journey a lot smoother and easier, especially at the beginning.

Determine What Kind of Vegan You Aspire to Be

The first thing you need to do is to determine the kind of vegan you want to be. By definition, being a vegan means not consuming or using any products which come from animals. But will you choose to continue eating honey? Will you continue eating wild fish? Will you continue eating eggs?

All of these decisions lie with you. If you choose to eliminate all animal-based food products, great! If not, think long and hard about the reasons why you have chosen to eliminate some types of food while maintaining others.

No matter what your reason is for going vegan, you must first find out the kind of vegan you want to be. This gives you a better idea of what you must do and what your long-term vegan goals are. Here are the basic kinds of vegans for you to determine where you think you fit in best:

1. **Ethical**

   A lot of vegans make this choice because they want to live a lifestyle that's more compassionate and caring. These vegans believe that animal exploitation must come to an end, which is why they also expand their lifestyle choices beyond their diets. Aside from eliminating animal and animal products from their diets, ethical vegans also avoid using products which are made from or are tested on animals. They also avoid visiting aquariums, zoos, and other establishments where animals are being exploited for entertainment and profit.

2. Raw

These vegans don't eat anything which has been heated or cooked. Therefore, their diets consist mainly of vegetables, fruits, grains, seeds, and nuts. Most people who choose this type of vegan diet are concerned about health benefits. For others, they choose to become raw vegans for spiritual reasons. There are some variations of this diet, which means that some raw vegans may still consume cooked meals at least once a day.

3. High-Carb, Low-Fat or HCLF

For these vegans, they consume huge quantities of carbohydrates in the form of grains, fruits, and vegetables. And they choose to consume as little fat as possible. HCLF vegans have different options depending on what they're looking for in the diet. Some choose to get their carbohydrates from pasta, rice, and potatoes, while others get the same nutrient from veggies and fruits. Nuts, seeds, and fruits like avocado contain essential healthy fats, but HCLF consume smaller quantities of these.

4. **Junk Food Vegan:** These vegans eat whatever they desire as long as animals were not harmed in the process. While it isn't the healthiest path, it is an ethical one.

5. **Environmentally Conscious**

   Finally, there are those who choose to go vegan in order to make their own contribution to the environment. Since mass consumption of dairy and meat products causes a lot of damage to the environment, some people choose to become vegans, so they don't contribute to this destruction. Environmentally conscious vegans are those who want to cut their carbon footprint down in hopes that other people make this choice too for the sake of our planet.

These are the most common and most basic types of vegan diets you can choose to become. Before you decide, you must think about your own reasons for going vegan. Then you can easily determine what kind of vegan you will become.

Don't Starve Yourself Just to Lose

Weight

I have been told stories of former vegans that reverted to eating meat because according to them, "it is food meant for rabbits and veganism is the same as starvation." As I have said, it depends on you. You can decide to adopt a balanced diet containing adequate quantities of fats, proteins, carbs, minerals, and vitamins or you can consume strictly uncooked foods, although this choice might result in complications like protein deficiency. Vegans who decide to restrict their dietary intake to vegetables and fruits can hardly follow through with the plant-based lifestyle. The reason being is that, this is not a balanced meal and once this routine has been established, they feel fatigued all the time, have low energy, and their muscle mass reduces.

The same thing happens with a non-vegan diet. With regards to this instance, we would not be discussing the effects of consuming animal products. Think about a non-vegan limiting their diet to meat exclusively. This implies that they would be getting a lot of protein. This will be an unbalanced diet. This individual would experience tiredness and inability to concentrate due to their insufficient intake of carbs.

If your goal is to lose weight and maintain a healthy weight on a vegan diet, eliminating meat and other animal products will already make a huge impact for you.

Make weight-loss part of your plan as you start your vegan journey. Then you can plan your diet in such a way that you eat a balanced diet where you get all the nutrients you need sans from plant-based food sources which promote weight loss. If you want to stick with veganism, starving yourself isn't the answer. Instead, you must change your eating habits to help you shed those unwanted pounds.

This will help keep you motivated since you will still be eating tasty and interesting foods as you approach your target weight. Then when you've reached your goal, continue following your vegan diet and try mixing things up to make your meals more enjoyable!

To sum it all up, becoming a vegan does not mean that you should starve yourself. The proper way is to provide your body with its requirements so that it would "function" while you benefit morally with your choices.

Start by Being a "Vegetarian for Now"

If you think you won't be able to handle being a vegan right away, you can try this step. A lot of vegans choose to become "vegetarian for now" as this makes the transition easier. If you've started with vegetarianism and you're thinking about taking it a step further and going vegan, then you're already well on your way!

If you're thinking about taking this baby step now, congratulations!

However, if you experience any setbacks, try to avoid compensating the lack of meat by consuming more eggs and cheese. Just because you're craving for meat, this doesn't mean you should over-indulge on eggs and cheese. Instead, give mock meats a try. As we've discussed, there are a lot of options to choose from. After some time, when you already feel more comfortable with being a vegetarian, you can try starting your vegan journey in the same way: By taking things one day at a time.

You Can Also Try Being a "Vegan for a Day"

Speaking of taking things one day at a time...

Another step you may take to help you succeed in your vegan journey is to try it out by being a "vegan for a day." This is effective because it's like you're telling your brain, "Okay, I'm just going to try this new thing out for one day." This makes it a lot easier than to think about being a vegan for the rest of your life. Start a tradition to make it easier for you to reach your goals one chunk at a time. For instance, you may try starting a tradition of "Meatless Monday" where you only practice veganism on this day.

Just take things one day at a time. Enjoy different types of plant-based meals and dishes one day each week. Keep trying foods from restaurants or different recipes until you find the ones which you enjoy the most. If this day falls on a special occasion, don't worry about it. Just move your vegan day to the next day.

Starting off by being too restrictive or too hard on yourself will ensure your failure. Even if you have no choice but to break the tradition you've set, that's okay. There's always another day. Doing this makes your journey a more positive one. Each time you're able to get through the whole day without consuming any non-vegan fare, celebrate this accomplishment. Soon, you'll notice that it's easier to start choosing vegan foods even on your non-vegan days.

Ditch Your Old Habits One at a Time

Whether you plan to start off by being vegetarian, you choose to become a vegan for a day, or you want to dive right into veganism, this step will help you out. The idea behind ditching your old habits one at a time is to ensure that the process happens gradually. That way, it would be kind of like playing a game accomplishing one level at a time. There will be habits which are harder to break so you may have to take more time to deal with these. Then there are those habits which are easy to get rid of so they would seem like nothing but bonus levels.

For instance, you can start by getting rid of the type of meat you don't eat as much as the others. For me, it was pork. Although I used to love meat, I was never a huge fan of pork. So that's where I started. I went from eating pork rarely to not eating pork at all. Then I stopped eating beef, milk and other dairy products, chicken and seafood, and, finally, cheese. That was where I struggled most because I used to love cheese so much.

Don't worry about how you tackle the elimination of these habits. Since it's your own choice and your own journey, it means that you'll be setting the rules too. You can take as little or as much time to get rid of your habits until you have finally transitioned into being a vegan.

Keeping a Food Diary

This is another great step to take as you start on your

vegan lifestyle journey. In fact, keeping a journal works for different types of diets because it helps make you more aware of the things you are eating each day. When you keep a journal, take down notes about the foods that you eat and how you feel after each meal. In doing this, you'll start noticing some patterns emerging depending on your food choices. For instance, some types of food make you feel fuller for a longer time. Then there are some which make you feel hungry after just a couple of hours.

Keeping a journal is especially useful if one of your goals is to lose weight. Through the journal, you can determine which foods promote weight loss by making you feel full for a longer time. Also, you can keep tabs on the portions of your meals. This gives you a better idea of your eating patterns and in which areas you can make some improvements. Several studies have shown that those who keep a journal have a higher chance of losing weight compared to those who just "wing it."

But in terms of starting a diet or food journal, how does this help you stick to your vegan diet? The most important purpose of such a journal is for you to be more aware of what you're eating. Also, when you go back to review your journal, you will be able to use it to make observations about your diet, such as:

- Do you tend to eat even when you're not feeling hungry? If so, what types of food do you eat?

- Whenever you're craving for something, do you eat that food right away?

- Do you have a tendency towards emotional eating?

- How much food are you eating? Do you eat enough at each meal, or do you still feel hungry after eating?

- Do certain foods make you feel tired or sleepy?

- Do you have a tendency towards overeating? If so, what types of food do you tend to consume in excess?

- How do you feel after you eat different kinds of food? Pay special attention to the new vegan foods which you're introducing to your diet.

- How fast do you chew your food? Do you just gobble everything down or do you take time to savor every bite? You can get this information by including your eating times in your journal.

- Are you influenced by the people you eat with? Do they have an effect on your own eating habits? This is very important, especially if you live with non-vegans. It would become very difficult for you to make the transition if you're easily influenced by your dining companions.

These are just some information and observations you

may record in your journal. But just like your vegan journey, creating and maintaining your food diary is all up to you. Therefore, you can make it as simple or as detailed as you want it to be. The important thing is that keeping a journal can help you make realizations about your eating habits. It can also motivate you and make you feel more empowered to start making changes in your diet.

Give up or Reduce the Consumption of Dairy

For would-be vegans, this is one of the most difficult parts of making the change. In fact, I remember how hard this part was for me too, especially since I absolutely loved cheese. Looking back, I can now admit that I was actually *addicted* to cheese. Although back then, you couldn't get me to admit it.

Cheese addiction is a real thing. It's not just something vegans invented to make non-vegans feel bad! But how does one get addicted to cheese?

When you eat cheese, the protein contained in the milk known as casein is converted to casomorphin. It is not coincidental that this is pronounced similar to morphine. This is because they are both opiates. This is one of nature's way of making young mammals addicted to milk, so they would not be able to resist the urge to go back for more, which helps them develop and become healthy to procreate.

Cows grow a lot bigger than us humans. This is because their milk also contains higher amounts of casein. Milk produced by humans only contains about 2.7 grams of casein for each liter. But for milk produced by cows, it contains up to 26 grams of the protein. This is a huge difference!

Now consider this: In order to make a single pound of cheese, manufacturers use 10 pounds of milk. This means that the cheese you love so much is chock full of casein which, after consumption, gets converted to casomorphin which gives the cheese its addictive quality. This is why a lot of people just can't seem to give up ice cream, milk, and cheese. In more severe cases, people actually experience withdrawal symptoms when they quit cheese abruptly, such as depression, extreme cravings, headaches, and more.

To make things worse, you can find cheese everywhere! It's sprinkled over pasta, used in baking, placed as a topping for pizzas and burgers; the list goes on. So, if you're like me (at least, the past me), giving cheese and dairy up will be a challenge. But look at where I am now! I can successfully and confidently say that I have kicked this addiction, which means you can too!

Also, another piece of good news is that there are a lot of excellent vegan alternatives for cheese, milk, and other dairy products. Furthermore, various brands are also coming up with their own alternative products to please the appetites of vegans all over the world. For instance, the famous ice cream brand, Ben & Jerry has launched a whole series of non-dairy ice cream. Hooray for us!

Being a Vegan at Home

The fear of failing while eating outside is what prevents a lot of people from adopting the vegan lifestyle. To be honest, it difficult. Think about being on the road and you might have to get food from the gas station. Muffins, protein bars, and hot dogs are the only things they have. As previously stated, you don't want to starve yourself.

In time, you will become experienced and knowledgeable enough to foresee and make plans for unforeseen circumstances and you will not have any difficulty with sticking to your vegan lifestyle, irrespective to where you might be.

However, you can start by committing to eat plant-based foods when you are at home and when you are on the road, you can eat whatever is suitable.

Slowly, you would stop regarding animal foods as tempting. Have confidence in yourself. The decision is yours to make and the journey is yours to bear.

Living in a Non-Vegan Home

Finally, you should also come up with a plan on how you will remain vegan while living in a non-vegan home. Again, this is entirely possible because this is my current situation. Although I haven't convinced my family to go vegan, I have introduced them to a lot of vegan foods which now, they really enjoy.

Don't be afraid of going vegan just because the rest of your household isn't. Although you may have to explain a couple of things to them, this doesn't mean that they will love you any less because you have decided to give up certain types of food. As long as you don't push your lifestyle on them, you won't have to worry about causing problems in your home.

For this last step, make sure that you prepare yourself adequately. If you will always be dining with non-vegans, this means that temptation will always be present. You need a really strong will to avoid reaching out for those dishes which you used to love. To help ease your situation, you should match those tasty dishes with scrumptious vegan dishes of your own. That way, you will still be enjoying your own meal even though you don't get to have what your dining companions are having.

It's all about convincing yourself to stick with the lifestyle choice you've decided to make. And if you employ all the other steps which we have discussed, making the change won't be as difficult. Over time, you'll notice that you don't see this animal or animal product foods as appealing. Just remember to take it easy on yourself so as not to make this journey harder than it has to be.

Chapter 17: Environmental Reasons for Becoming a Vegan

By now, you may already have your own reason for becoming a vegan. Things are starting to get clearer, and thanks to the last chapter, you also have a number of actionable steps to help you start your vegan journey. But the benefits of being a vegan don't end there. For some people, their main reason for becoming a vegan is that they want to make a difference for the benefit of our planet.

This is another great reason for becoming a vegan. By going vegan, you stop supporting the animal food industry. Although this might not seem like a significant step to others, it actually makes a huge impact, especially if more people decide to make this same choice. But how does being a vegan help the environment? Let's find out.

Greenhouse Gases

Some people may wonder how dishes such as lasagna, burgers, or fried chicken may harm the environment. The fact is, all livestock farmed in factories give off huge amounts of methane gas. This is a type of greenhouse gas that's a lot more powerful compared to CO_2. If more people go vegan, there won't be a huge demand for breeding and raising animals in factory farms. This helps reduce the methane gas that is given off into the atmosphere, which, in turn, helps in a huge way.

For smaller animals such as lambs, chickens, pigs, and turkey, the issue is not centered around methane, but on the electricity resources and power that is required for slaughterhouses, factories, farms and even transportation systems to function effectively.

Based on a study by the United Nations titled *Livestock's Long Shadow*, animal farming results in the production of more greenhouse gases than the various forms of transportation across the world (UN, Livestock's Long Shadow, 2006).

Land and Rainforests

I love watching '*Our Planet*' on Netflix. Watching and realizing how beautiful this planet is, how unique the species living on it are and how everything is connected, and functions so perfectly well, to me, is a profound experience. What I don't like about the documentary is how at the end of each episode I get to see that it's us humans, who destroy forests, rivers, oceans and deserts.

In order to grow crops and grains for all of the livestock, the agricultural animal industry makes use of around 30% of the planet's land that's ice-free. If that's not bad enough, rainforests are being cleared of trees in order to have enough space for grazing and growing these crops.

Research conducted by the University of Oxford in 2018 discovered that the least significant dairy product and meat resulted in greater damage to the environment compared to the most significant vegetable and grain production. For instance, peas require 36 times less land compared to low significant beef.

This research also discovered that if everyone across the world cuts out dairy products and meat, the use of farms worldwide could be lowered by 75% and create a land size that is equal to the combined size of the European Union, China, U.S., and Australia ALTOGETHER.

Animals eat 30% of all grains and 60% of all barley, soybeans, and corn, so lowering the intake of animal products would create additional land that could be used for other purposes.

In 2018, some researchers at the University of Wisconsin-Madison contrasted the land required by each animal-based food product in the United States to a nutritionally equivalent substitute that was plant-based. They discovered that substituting animal-based products with plant-based products could support 350 million more people. They also discovered that land that generated 100 grams of protein consumed from plants produced only 25 grams of consumable protein from dairy, 50 grams of chicken, 60 grams of consumable protein from eggs, 10 grams from pigs and a mere 4 grams from beef.[2]

Raising and Breeding Animals Consumes Water

It is so sad that clean drinking water is not accessible to about 783 million people in the world, whereas animal farming consumes about 30% of the drinking water available on Earth.[3]

According to PETA, in the US, almost half of the water is used by factory farms for raising livestock and other animals for consumption. The situation has become so bad that PETA even claims that one person would be able

[2] Shepon, A., Eshel, G., Noor, E., & Milo, R. (2018). The opportunity cost of animal based diets exceeds all food losses. *Proceedings of the National Academy of Sciences, 115*(15), 3804-3809.

[3] Gerbens-Leenes, P., Mekonnen, M., & Hoekstra, A. (2013). The water footprint of poultry, pork and beef: A comparative study in different countries and production systems. *Water Resources And Industry, 1-2*, 25-36. doi: 10.1016/j.wri.2013.03.001

to save more water by not consuming one pound of meat than by not taking a shower for six months![4] They've come up with calculations where they discovered that factory farms require about 2,400 gallons of water just to produce one pound of meat! But for farmers to grow one pound of vegetables, they would only require 25 gallons of water. That's a huge difference, isn't it?

A research that was conducted in 2016 and published in the Science of the Total Environment contrasted the traditional Mediterranean diets to vegan diets, animal-based diets, and pesco-vegetarian diets. They discovered that vegan diets consumed the lowest quantity of water.[5]

Marine Pollution

Harvey Blatt wrote in his book titled What You Don't Know About What You Eat, that farm animals in the United States generate 1.5 billion tons of manure which is 130% more waste that is produced by Americans (the population of Americans is about 300 million). In past

---

4 PETA. (2019). The Meat Industry Wastes Water. Retrieved from https://www.peta.org/blog/meat-industry-wastes-water/

5 Vanham, D., del Pozo, S., Pekcan, A., Keinan-Boker, L., Trichopoulou, A., & Gawlik, B. (2016). Water consumption related to different diets in Mediterranean cities. Science of the Total Environment, 573, 96-105.

years, this has posed a very big problem and has been a major contaminant in the water. Aside from this, the water also gets polluted from the antibiotics, hormones, and chemicals given to the different kinds of animals.

Pollution and Environmental Racism

Not only does agricultural animal industry harm us indirectly through polluting our planet, but it also harm households directly. The Sierra Club reports that Dairy farms and Hog farms generate a large quantity of waste, which is reserved and sprayed on the fields.[6]

When waste is sprayed frequently, it permeates the soil and penetrates the aquifer and close streams and rivers. This also converts fecal matter into aerosols and results in the generation of poisonous chemicals that are carried by the wind into nearby houses with an unbearable stench that forces residents to remain indoors. Most of these homes are owned by African American whose homes and

---

[6] Skolnick, A. (2017). The CAFO Industry's Impact on the Environment and Public Health. Retrieved from https://www.sierraclub.org/sierra/2017-2-march-april/feature/cafo-industrys-impact-environment-and-public-health

wells to have been contaminated with hog wastes for decades.

Their grievances about the detrimental effects to their health have been unanswered by the statehouse in North Carolina for about 30 years. This has made it a very evident case of environmental racism at the cost of human lives.

Based on what was said by an individual residing close to the hog waste lagoons, the Sierra Club quotes:

The presence of hog waste here is as frequent as raindrops. If we are outside, we breathe in hog wastes it also permeates our houses indoors. We cannot hold family gatherings or cook-outs like in the past because we cannot predict the moment when the odor might decide to come. When it becomes high, it makes your eyes burn.

The Solution

As you can see, those "simple" and "innocent" dishes which contain meat aren't what they seem. A lot of processes go into the production of these animal-based foods. In order for them to reach our plate, farmers, manufacturers, and other workers in the agricultural animal industry use a lot of our planet's resources and pollute our environment too.

Modifying your diet can make a great change in your life. It is a known fact that cars that run on gas are uneconomical and incompetent, and the same can be said about dairy and meat production.

Utilizing energy-saving bulbs or changing to an electric car is just not enough if all people keep consuming burgers and steaks. The only solution is to reduce the amount of meat eaten.

By eating a plant-based diet, you are helping to sustain the ecosystem.

Chapter 18: Cruelty-Free Living

- Going Beyond What You Eat

Apart from consuming animals and animal products, a lot of vegans go beyond this and try to live a life that's completely cruelty-free. To give you an idea of what animals have to endure, here are some examples:

- Some animals are kept as pets, but instead of treating them like a member of the family, these animals are being abused.

- Rodents, rabbits, and other kinds of animals are used to test the safety of products.

- Different kinds of animal fighting activities.

- Kitten and puppy mills.

- Some people hoard animals to "save" them, but then, these animals are kept in cramped spaces where they live the same lives as those in factory farms.

- A lot of animals are being exploited for entertainment purposes like in the circus, in resorts, and more.

- Some animals are also bred and raised for their fur.

What About My Leather Shoes?

Picture this: What if you decide to go vegan, but you own tons of fur coats, leather shoes, leather bags, belts and so on. Does this mean that you should get rid of all your belongings which have been made from animals' fur or skin right away?

The short answer is, no.

Part of being a vegan is being more compassionate. But when you try and get to know some vegans, you'll discover that we're also reasonable people. Just because you've decided on a vegan lifestyle, that doesn't mean that you should rid yourself of everything you've owned before you became vegan just to align with your values. This is especially true if these items have sentimental value. Deciding not to buy any more of these animal products is already an excellent step to take if you want to align your lifestyle with your values. When you go shopping, you can look for alternative products which are comfortable, which look pretty, and, most importantly, which aren't made from innocent animals.

If you're wondering what the big deal is with leather purses, fur coats, and similar items, let me paint a picture for you. Consider this: To make a single coat, manufacturers need around 20 foxes, 80 squirrels or 30 raccoons. We've talked about the miserable lives of the animals raised for food. Now apply the same situation to other kinds of animals, but this time, the animals are raised for their fur, their skin, or merely for the purpose of animal testing. The good news is that more and bigger brands and top designers are starting to refuse using leather and fur for their shoes and clothing lines.

Another bit of good news for you is that we are living in a time when it's very easy to be a vegan. No matter what your budget is, you can purchase countless cruelty-free items which still look classy and stylish. Thanks to the utilization of eco-friendly plant-based materials as well as new technology, we have so many different options for cruelty-free shoes, vegan clothes, and even cosmetics. In fact, some products that closely resemble leather in appearance are actually synthetic. With this in mind, it's a good idea to check labels just to be sure.

The bottom line is this: Don't stress yourself out if you want part of your vegan journey to include a transition into a cruelty-free lifestyle. Going vegan is a process whether it involves your diet or the other aspects of your life. For this process, you can also use the actionable steps (just make a few tweaks to them) from Chapter 16 to "veganize" your closet. That way, you won't have to see this change as a negative or difficult process which you must endure. Just have fun as you gradually replace one pair at a time.

Chapter 19: The Unexpected Benefits of Going Vegan

Apart from the obvious health and ethical benefits, going vegan also comes with a number of surprising benefits you should look forward to. The great thing about veganism is that it has the potential to improve different aspects of your life, not just your health. Consider these unexpected benefits of going vegan:

Compassion for Others

The longer you stay a vegan, the more compassionate you learn to be. This value comes naturally to vegans. Part of your vegan journey is learning more about how animals are treated in the food industry. This is why I included the "tough chapters" in this book. The more you learn the truth about animal cruelty, the more you will understand why vegans just won't stand for it!

And this compassion doesn't only apply to animals. You will also start learning how to become more compassionate towards other people. As the people around you learn to accept your new lifestyle, you will learn to appreciate their efforts. Then, when you encounter other people who are different for you, this makes you feel accepting and compassionate towards them too.

Compassion for Yourself

I've mentioned how you shouldn't be too hard on yourself as you embark on your journey into veganism. This is an important part of the process so as not to make the whole experience negative for you. Throughout your vegan journey, you will also start learning how to be compassionate towards yourself.

When you encounter challenges which you find difficult to overcome, give yourself time. Don't rush things. If you fail, like if you crave for meat and you end up having one burger just to satisfy that craving, don't worry about it too much. Take responsibility for your own actions and always remember that tomorrow is a new day to do better!

Health Consciousness

It is very common for new vegans to carry out a lot of research to ensure they get all the essential nutrients required for their bodies. They are susceptible to falling for common notions such as the belief that they might lack iron, B12, and protein if they become vegan. In fact, by eating more plant-based foods and less saturated fat, you end being a healthier person. Another benefit to veganism is that your body would carry out its functions more effectively because you are consuming foods with more nutritional value.

As your bodily functions improve, you have a much better feel for what's going on within. I for one can feel energy surging through my body than I ever have before. I can't consume alcohol as I used to since becoming a vegan and when I use new medications, I feel their effects a lot more than I used to. This may just be what it means to become an adult and is simply the product of paying more attention to my body, but I choose to believe these differences are the result of my new diet. Another thing to note is the fact that vegans in general claim to have reached a state of mental clarity with their brains feeling less "foggy." Hopefully with a vegan diet, your mind will also benefit from the nutrients you're taking in.

Being Aligned with Your Values

Another thing you may discover once you become vegan is that it aligns well with your values. This is especially true if your main reason for becoming a vegan is ethics. If ever since, you have felt strongly about the mistreatment of animals, transitioning into veganism helps you "practice what you preach."

Even in terms of health, veganism can provide this benefit. If you're all about health and fitness, the good news is that veganism can help you become a healthier person too! As long as you know why you want to become vegan, you can align this new lifestyle with your own values.

Connecting with Like-Minded People

This is one of the unexpected benefits that I particularly enjoy. Since becoming a vegan, I have met some incredible like-minded people. It's easy to meet these people as long as you know where to look (more on this later). There's just something so satisfying with meeting, interacting, and building friendships with other vegans.

You can think of these people as your "support system," especially when your loved ones aren't really enthusiastic about your lifestyle choice. Veganism allows you to broaden your horizon in terms of meeting new and interesting people so you can build connections which will last a lifetime!

Stop Getting Bloated

One great thing about the vegan diet is that you will learn how to eat certain types of food which will help you stop getting bloated. Bloating is a common problem which is usually caused by the foods we eat. Although some people do experience belly bloat when they go vegan, this can be easily avoided by consuming these foods:

- Warm water with lemon

- Digestive herbs and spices such as mint, ginger, chamomile, cilantro, and parsley.

- Foods which are rich in vitamin B6 such as bananas, potatoes, and walnuts.

- Foods which are rich in magnesium such as leafy greens, whole grains, and nuts.

- Celery.

- Watermelon.

- Chia seeds.

Stop Feeling Sleepy and Tired After Eating

The vegan diet encourages you to eat plant-based food sources, most of which are rich in essential vitamins, minerals, and nutrients. If you have noticed how you always felt tired and sleepy in the past after each meal, you may notice that this happens less and less now that you're vegan.

This is because a lot of the foods included in the vegan diet provide you with all the energy you need to stay happy, healthy, and strong. There are many types of energy-boosting vegan foods to choose from allowing you to face each day with enthusiasm.

No More Constipation

Finally, the vegan diet also helps prevent constipation. This is mainly because of the high fiber content of plants. Aside from this, there are other ways the vegan diet can help you prevent constipation, including:

- A softer consistency of stool.

- An increased frequency of your bowel movements.

- An increase in your intestinal motility along with a decrease in the transit time of your fecal matter through your intestines.

Chapter 20: How to Stay Motivated as a Vegan

I've noticed a powerful, soul arising urge to adopt a more conscious way of life among vegans. We see the value in our actions, and we feel compassion. We often try to move forward with a burning passion that it feels like we could set the world ablaze... only to discover that our world doesn't agree with our cause which is to be better humans. When faced with opposition, it can be very challenging. It is very sad when you come to realize that this world is not exactly vegan-friendly. Things don't have to be this hard and we can make them easier by preparing ourselves ahead of time and choosing to view things from an advantageous perspective.

I felt alone when I decided to adopt a vegan lifestyle a couple of years ago. I alleviated that loneliness by learning how to integrate my new beliefs and lifestyle into the non-vegan world. To get things up and running in my new vegan life, I subscribed to vegan blogs, joined Facebook groups and forums, and proceeded to read every single issue. Just knowing that there were other people already living the vegan life had an immensely positive impact on my transition. Time was one thing I had in abundance and I spent it trying to figure things out. Sometimes I had to read 5-10 articles a day to figure something out.

Choosing to become a vegan is a long, fulfilling, and enjoyable process. No matter how long you remain a vegan, there will always be opportunities for you to learn new things. Fortunately, it is very easy to find relevant information today. The internet is becoming increasingly popular and by making use of it, I've been able to enjoy the most delicious vegan cuisines from various parts of the world. Most times, I travel due to my work and one of the first things I do when I get to a new place is to look for places that caters to my vegan lifestyle.

Luckily, veganism becomes more and more popular. The fact that more people are making the transition makes me very excited. I still hear stories from friends, family and fellow travelers about the difficulties of remaining vegan. So, I have some friendly tips to help ensure that your new lifestyle continues to go smoothly.

Finding Like-Minded People to Keep You Motivated

This tip may sound familiar to you. That's because I just discussed something similar in the previous chapter. One unexpected benefit of being a vegan is that you're able to connect with like-minded people. This is highly beneficial too because these people who share the same values as you and who are on the same journey as you can keep you motivated.

When you encounter people who have been vegans for a long time, you can learn a lot from them. Conversely, if you meet people who are also starting their vegan journey, you can swap stories and share advice on how you overcame certain challenges. Either way, building friendships with like-minded people will inspire you more to stick with this life choice you decided to make.

Find Inspiration on Pinterest

Have you ever tried browsing through the different Pinterest boards? If you have, you would know that you can get a wealth of ideas and information which will prove useful to you. If you haven't tried visiting Pinterest yet, I highly recommend it!

Here, you will find tons of inspiration. From vegan recipes to ideas for vegan food combinations, vegan party ideas, and more, there's a lot for you to discover. So, if you're feeling particularly challenged or overwhelmed and you don't know where to turn to, give Pinterest a try. When you've become more adept at being a vegan, and you've discovered some amazing recipes, dishes or ideas, share them on Pinterest too! That way, you can also serve as an inspiration to others.

Find Inspiration on YouTube

Speaking of finding inspiration online, you can also find a lot of inspiration on YouTube. Simply browse YouTube and you may be able to find some incredible videos which will keep you motivated. There are tons of channels out there where people share their inspiring stories of how they made the transition to veganism.

Earthling Ed

One example of a motivational channel on YouTube is the one by "Earthing Ed." He is a vegan activist who spreads the idea of veganism in a positive way by sharing compassion and love. In his videos, he often speaks to non-vegans who disagree with him. Ed is known for his strength to stay calm and rational, and for asking the right questions.

His project 'Land of Hope and Glory' is a free documentary that shows the animals go through. You can watch it for free by visiting www.landofhopeandglory.org. To learn more about Ed and his further projects, go to www.earthlinged.com.

To join his supporter community by becoming a patron, visit www.patreon.com/earthlinged.

Joey Carbstrong

Joey is an animal right activist who once was an alcohol and drug user as well as ex-member of a criminal gang. This part of his life landed him in prison. After he left the gang life and became vegan, he felt it was his duty to speak up and help the less fortunate.

If you want to hear his message and open your heart, find him on YouTube and visit his website at www.joeycarbstrong.com. You can learn how to support Joey's work, and help him, help the animals by going to www.patreon.com/joeycarbstrong.

Mic the Vegan

Mic's YouTube channel covers variety of topics from the health effect of eating a plant-based diet and the environmental impact of eating animal products, to the phenomenon of animal exploitation. Mic is a vegan science writer who uses his humor to debunks myths about veganism.

You can check on him and his work by going to his website www.micthevegan.com and you can also become a supporter by visiting www.patreon.com/micthevegan.

The Tofu Goddess

On her YouTube channel, Leanna, also known as The

Tofu Goddess, talks about everything from vegan food to pet ownership and freeganism. She provides a dose of much needed compassion and realism. Her channel is worth following. You can find Leanna also on Instagram, by searching for 'tofu.goddess.'

Apart from these motivational channels, you will also find a lot of inspiration for cooking, planting your own produce, how to find the healthiest food options in supermarkets, and so on! Whatever you're looking for, there's a good chance that you'll find it on YouTube.

Other Tips for Staying Motivated

Becoming a vegan is easier said than done. As I've mentioned several times in this book, becoming a vegan is a lifestyle choice which, at times, can feel frustrating. The good news is that there are so many ways you can stay motivated. As long as you want to continue being a vegan, you will always be able to find inspiration. Here are more tips for you:

- **Learn as much as you can about being a vegan.** The more informed you are, the more motivated you will be.

- **Know the difference between "can" and**

"want." Just because you "can" do something - like eat animals - this doesn't mean that you "want to" or "should" do it.

- **Clean up your home, especially your kitchen.** This is an important motivational step, especially if you want to avoid temptation.

- **Call the restaurant prior going.** When you decide to eat out with friends, call the restaurant ahead of the time to ensure they have vegan dishes. While this may seem awkward, it is far better than getting to the restaurant and not having a clue of what you should eat or whether their dishes are vegan.

- **Make being Vegan "normal."** Everyone started accepting my new lifestyle when I stopped being bothered by their opinions about my eating habits. People are uncomfortable when they are faced with views that threatens the very foundation of their lifestyle (in this case, consuming meat and animal products). At first, it's best to be content with your lifestyle, but feel compassion for others. People are more likely to question their own choices if you are satisfied with your eating habits and you are not judgmental of theirs. I used to think by informing people of the benefits of a vegan lifestyle, they will incorporate the lifestyle into their daily lives. Unfortunately, this is not the case with most people. Don't let that get you down though. Just keep doing your thing. You'll be the first person people turn to when they need directions for conscious eating if they respect you and your choices. Now, I noticed a lot of people around me are very interested in my lifestyle and they have many questions. Being vegan has a way of rubbing off on people.

- **Forgive yourself.** You can't put a price on self-forgiveness! A vegan lifestyle is a path of compassion and kindness. You should ensure that some of that compassion is pointed towards you. If you fail, keep in mind that you can always try again. You learn to forgive yourself when you slip up. You should also learn to celebrate your little achievements along the way. By being even a little vegan, you are on a much better path than if you were to give up. And this is what we will be talking about in the next which also happens to be the last chapter of this book.

Chapter 21: What Happens If You Fail?

There is nothing so wretched or foolish as to anticipate misfortunes.
What madness it is in your expecting evil before it arrives!

\- Seneca

After everything you've learned from this book, you should know by now that if you fail, you shouldn't be too hard on yourself. Remember, as long as you want to change, you will be able to do it.

But fear of failure is a different story. If you don't want to become a vegan because you're afraid that you'll fail at being one, it's time to change how you think. Most people who decided to become vegans had doubts and fears. But they made the change anyway. As one who has successfully made the transition, I hope you believe me when I say that your thoughts are a lot scarier than the actual process.

I myself had experienced failure several times throughout my vegan transition. But I kept reminding myself that failure is part of the process, and I am strong enough to pick myself up and keep going. If I can do it, so can you!

If doubts are plaguing your mind and preventing you from taking that all-important first step, let me help calm your mind. Here are some of the most common reasons why people fail at becoming a vegan and how you can deal with each of them.

Preparing Vegan Meals Takes Time

I won't tell you that this isn't true. Preparing vegan meals does take time, but only at the beginning. Since you'll be changing your diet, you will have to learn how to prepare new kinds of meals, recipes, and dishes which fit into your new diet. But the more you learn how to make these dishes, and the more you practice, the faster and more efficient you become.

If the preparation intimidates you, then you may want to start meal prepping. This is when you set one day each week to prepare all the meals you will be eating for the rest of the week. This is where Pinterest and Google come in handy. In these sites, you will find a lot of vegan meal prep ideas to save time, energy, and money too! Meal prepping allows you to have all your meals ready from breakfast all the way to dinner.

164

Meal prep involves planning, shopping for ingredients, preparing and cooking your meals, and storing everything you've prepared. This is an excellent strategy because it can help keep you motivated, too, especially when you see how easy it is and how well it works for you.

It's Hard to Find Restaurants or Food Options When You're On the Go

This is another reason why people fail at being vegans. As soon as they enter restaurants, they end up ordering non-vegan fare because they don't have a choice. Although this may have been true in the past, this doesn't have to be a common excuse now. These days, there are so many websites and apps you can use to find recommendations of vegan restaurants and food options in your area.

Do your research, and you'll be surprised at how many local restaurants actually offer vegan-friendly options! Even if you don't use these apps, there are certain types of restaurants which usually offer vegan options. These include the more "ethnic" dining options such as those which offer Middle Eastern, Ethiopian, Mexican, Italian, and Indian cuisine. But if you're interested in using apps to help you out, you may try Happy Cow, Yelp, and Eater.

Living with a Non-Vegan Partner

For a lot of people, this is a tough one. Whether you're currently in a relationship with a non-vegan who doesn't want to change, or you're interested in dating non-vegans, the best thing for you to do is, to be honest, and communicate openly. Talk about how you're planning to become a vegan and what this means. Have a conversation about the changes which will happen in your life and how these may impact your partner.

You must also set some ground rules to keep your relationship healthy while still being able to stick with your diet. After you've had "the talk" and your partner is okay with you being a vegan and with the rules you've set, then you can start implementing those rules. It may be challenging at first, but, trust me, things will get better.

When you're feeling more comfortable with your non-vegan partner, when you've found your "groove," then you may want to share some of the best aspects of veganism with your partner. This doesn't mean that you should talk about animal abuse and cruelty. Instead, make this a positive experience for your partner by cooking delicious vegan meals and sharing your own experiences about how much you're enjoying the health benefits of being a vegan. The important thing here is not to push your lifestyle on your partner. Be open, share your thoughts, and be as encouraging as you possibly can. This will make the transition easier on both of you.

It's Challenging to Remain Vegan while Traveling

This is another challenging situation. I've also experienced this at the beginning of my vegan journey. While you're on the road, you may find it extremely difficult to find plant-based or vegan-friendly foods, especially if your pit stops only include gas stations or diners which only offer unhealthy, non-vegan food choices.

In order to deal with this, the best thing to do is to prepare your own snacks to bring with you for the trip. Pack crackers, fruits, nuts, protein shakes, sandwiches, chocolate, and other vegan food items which you really enjoy. That way, even if you stop at a restaurant with no vegan options, you still have something to munch on without having to stray from your diet. When it comes to traveling, preparation is key.

Feeling Deprived at Parties or Restaurants

For this issue, some would-be vegans end up quitting because they always feel deprived. But this shouldn't be the case. Have a conversation with your family and with your closest friends. Explain to them that you plan to make a huge change in your life, but this doesn't mean that you don't want to spend time with them anymore just because they're non-vegan. Instead, talk about how much you would appreciate it if they consider your current food preferences when hosting parties or when choosing restaurants to dine at.

Don't be afraid to talk about this with your loved ones. Also, don't be too pushy. Just tell them about your new diet and answer any questions they may have about it. If you're planning to attend a non-vegan party, volunteer to bring a vegan dish or snack. The host will surely appreciate this, especially if you bring something interesting that everyone will enjoy. You don't have to be deprived. As long as you remain open and proactive, you will be able to find ways to feel happy and satisfied, no matter where you eat.

Conclusion: It's Time to Start Your Vegan Journey to Save Your Life!

So, there you have it, a short guide on how you can start your vegan journey and stick with it. There's no time like the present. Now that you've learned a lot about becoming a vegan and all the information is still fresh in your mind, this is the best time for you to take those baby steps into veganism.

Believe me when I say that this lifestyle choice will bring a lot of good things with it, especially in the long run. Even if you happen to experience some challenges along the way, don't feel discouraged. Take these as learning opportunities to help you grow. Before I end this book, let me leave you with a challenge: Think about everything you've read and try to come up with your own reason for why you want to become a vegan. As soon as you have a solid reason, you will find the inspiration to start your vegan journey to save your life. Good luck!

Bibliography

11 Vegan Foods That Are Complete Protein Sources |
PETA. (2019). Retrieved from
https://www.peta.org/living/food/complete-proteins-
vegan/

21 Things the Egg Industry Doesn't Want You to See |
PETA. (2019). Retrieved from
https://www.peta.org/features/egg-industry-cruelty/

3 Morally-Sobering Reasons Vegans Don't Eat Eggs.
(2019). Retrieved from
https://www.theplantway.com/why-vegans-dont-eat-
eggs/

32 Famous Athletes Who Are Vegan. (2019). Retrieved
from https://www.ranker.com/list/athletes-who-are-
vegan/people-in-sports?page=4

4 Easy Tips to Stay Motivated in a Vegan Diet. (2019).
Retrieved from https://www.lifehack.org/425670/4-
easy-tips-stay-motivated-vegan-diet

4 WAYS BEING VEGAN IS CHEAPER THAN EATING
MEAT | Vegan Blog | OhSheVegan. (2019). Retrieved
from https://www.ohshevegan.com/single-
post/2018/01/06/4-WAYS-BEING-VEGAN-IS-
CHEAPER-THAN-EATING-MEAT

6 Tips for Losing Weight on a Vegan Diet. (2019). Retrieved from https://vegnews.com/2018/6/6-tips-for-losing-weight-on-a-vegan-diet

7 Plant-Based Foods to Fight Belly Bloat | 22 Days Nutrition. (2019). Retrieved from https://www.22daysnutrition.com/blog/7-plant-based-foods-to-fight-belly-bloat

7 Reasons Why Going Vegan Failed The First Time. (2019). Retrieved from http://www.blackvegandiaries.com/blog/7-reasons-why-going-vegan-failed-the-first-time

Acidic Foods: What to Limit or Avoid. (2019). Retrieved from https://www.healthline.com/health/acid-foods-to-avoid

Akers, K. (2019). Truth-Force and Vegetarianism | Compassionate Spirit. Retrieved from https://www.compassionatespirit.com/wpblog/1998/01/01/truth-force-and-vegetarianism/

Alix, M. (2019). Why Vegetarians/Vegans Don't Eat Fish: There's More to it than Being Friends. Retrieved from https://www.hercampus.com/school/vanderbilt/why-vegetariansvegans-dont-eat-fish-theres-more-it-being-friends

Allen, P. (2019). What would happen if everyone went

vegan? Retrieved from
https://www.bbcgoodfood.com/howto/guide/what-would-world-look-if-everyone-went-vegan

Andrews, S. (2019). Didn't God put animals here for us to eat?. Retrieved from
https://humanelivingnet.net/2017/08/13/didnt-god-put-animals-here-for-us-to-eat/

Are organic plant-based foods better? – The Green Vegans. (2019). Retrieved from
https://thegreenvegans.com/are-organic-plant-based-foods-better/

Brocklehurst, R. (2019). HuffPost is now a part of Oath. Retrieved from
https://www.huffpost.com/entry/vegans-dont-eat-eggs_n_9622322

Cappiello, J. (2019). Vegan Dining Guide: Finding Your Best Restaurant Choices - Vegan.com. Retrieved from https://www.vegan.com/dining/

Capps, A. (2019). 16 Former Meat & Dairy Farmers Who Became Vegan Activists. Retrieved from
https://freefromharm.org/animal-products-and-ethics/former-meat-dairy-farmers-became-vegan-activists/

Chambers, G. (2019). Going vegan: How to cut down on meat and dairy. Retrieved from https://www.standard.co.uk/lifestyle/going-vegan-how-to-cutting-down-on-meat-dairy-a3988956.html

Coffin, E. (2019). HuffPost is now a part of Oath. Retrieved from https://www.huffpost.com/entry/why-do-vegans-eat-fake-me_b_3543316

Compassion- The Best Part of Being Vegan. (2019). Retrieved from http://fabulouslyvegan.com/compassionthebestpart/

DAVIS, M. (2019). SOY: THE MISUNDERSTOOD SUPERFOOD | WellSeek. Retrieved from https://wellseek.co/2016/11/30/soy-the-misunderstood-superfood/

Differences Between Omega-3 Fats From Plants and Marine Animals. (2019). Retrieved from https://articles.mercola.com/sites/articles/archive/2016/09/11/omega-3-from-plants-vs-marine-animals.aspx

Does The Vegan Diet Help The Environment? - Simply Quinoa. (2019). Retrieved from https://www.simplyquinoa.com/vegan-diet-help-environment/

Editorial, C. (2019). 5 Side Effects Of Eating Chicken You Need To Beware Of. Retrieved from https://www.curejoy.com/content/side-effects-of-eating-chicken/

English, N. (2019). 10 Complete Proteins Vegans Need to Know About. Retrieved from https://greatist.com/health/complete-vegetarian-proteins

Enochs, E. (2019). How to Stay Nourished When You're a Vegan Who Travels a Lot. Retrieved from https://chooseveg.com/blog/how-to-stay-nourished-when-youre-a-vegan-who-travels-a-lot/

Finding Your Tribe: How to Connect w/ Like Minded People - The Veggie Villager. (2019). Retrieved from https://www.theveggievillager.com/finding-your-tribe/

Fischer, K. (2019). the truth about the vegan diet. Retrieved from https://www.sheknows.com/health-and-wellness/articles/1020893/5-myths-about-going-vegan/

Funk, J. (2019). Food Network UK | TV Channel | Easy Recipes, TV Shows and Videos. Retrieved from https://www.foodnetwork.com/healthyeats/2009/09/different-kinds-of-mock-meats

Gerbens-Leenes, P., Mekonnen, M., & Hoekstra, A. (2013). The water footprint of poultry, pork and beef: A comparative study in different countries and production systems. Water Resources And Industry, 1-2, 25-36. doi: 10.1016/j.wri.2013.03.001

Gerson, J. (2019). Alberta's straight-talking, belligerent statesman launches his own era - Macleans.ca. Retrieved from https://www.macleans.ca/opinion/albertas-straight-talking-belligerent-statesman-launches-his-own-era/

Height, A. (2019). How to Use a Vegan Diet to Keep Your Body Alkaline. Retrieved from https://www.onegreenplanet.org/natural-health/how-to-use-a-vegan-diet-to-keep-your-body-alkaline/

Held, L. (2019). The China Study Summary: Everything you need to know | Well+Good. Retrieved from https://www.wellandgood.com/good-food/china-study-cheat-sheet-10-things-you-need-to-know/

Henry, A. (2019). What Does Organic Really Mean, and Is It Worth My Money?. Retrieved from https://lifehacker.com/what-does-organic-really-mean-and-is-it-worth-my-money-5941881

Here Are Just 12 Reasons Why Milk Is Bad for You | PETA Living. (2019). Retrieved from https://www.peta.org/living/food/reasons-stop-drinking-milk/

How to Be a Healthy Vegetarian. (2019). Retrieved from https://youngwomenshealth.org/2013/12/05/vegetarian-diet/

How to Survive as a Vegan in a Non-Vegan Household. (2019). Retrieved from https://www.onegreenplanet.org/lifestyle/how-to-survive-as-a-vegan-in-a-non-vegan-household/

Humane Farming Myth – Woodstock Sanctuary. (2019). Retrieved from http://woodstocksanctuary.org/learn/humane-farming-myth/

Humane Slaughter? - Humane Facts. (2019). Retrieved from https://humanefacts.org/humane-slaughter/

Imatome-Yun, N. (2019). The Standard American Diet is Even Sadder Than We Thought. Retrieved from https://www.forksoverknives.com/standard-american-diet-sadder-than-we-thought/#gs.bmtp81

Is Pork Bad for You? 4 Hidden Dangers. (2019). Retrieved from https://www.healthline.com/nutrition/is-pork-bad#section1

Kelley, J. (2019). The Benefits (and Limitations) of an Alkaline Diet - HUM Nutrition Blog. Retrieved from https://www.humnutrition.com/blog/alkaline-diet/

Krantz, R. (2019). 32 Celebrities You Didn't Know Were Totally Vegan. Retrieved from https://www.bustle.com/articles/149515-32-verified-currently-vegan-celebrities

Kurp, P. (2019). What About Vegan? (Taking Baby Steps) - Mainly Vegan. Retrieved from https://mainlyvegan.com/going-vegan-gradually/

Lang, R. (2019). The Lifecycle of the Dairy Cow. Retrieved from https://medium.com/@UnderdoneComics/the-lifecycle-of-the-dairy-cow-62578b022aea

Leo Galland MD: Unlock Your Health. (2019). Retrieved from http://drgalland.com/the-standard-american-diet-sad/

Levin, S. (2019). So(y) Misunderstood: What the research really says about soy | Vegan personal trainer | Online vegan fitness coach | Vegan coaching. Retrieved from https://www.karinainkster.com/single-post/2017/01/10/Soy-Misunderstood-What-the-research-really-says-about-soy

Loria, J. (2019). Here's the Problem With Humane Meat. Retrieved from https://mercyforanimals.org/heres-the-problem-with-humane-meat

Lupica, D. (2019). 6 Shocking Reasons You Should Stop Eating Chickens Now. Retrieved from https://www.plantbasednews.org/post/top-reasons-why-you-should-stop-eating-chicken

Marengo, K. (2019). Dairy alternatives: A guide to the best dairy substitutes. Retrieved from https://www.medicalnewstoday.com/articles/323411.ph

p

McCarthy, J., & Sanchez, E. (2019). 9 Ways Veganism Is Helping the Planet. Retrieved from https://www.globalcitizen.org/en/content/9-reasons-why-veganism-can-save-the-world/

McClelland, K. (2019). The Dirty Dozen: 12 Foods You Should Always Buy Organic. Retrieved from https://www.onegreenplanet.org/natural-health/vegan-health/the-dirty-dozen-12-foods-you-should-always-buy-organic/

Miles, A. (2019). Veganism as a Tool for Compassion - The Good Men Project. Retrieved from https://goodmenproject.com/featured-content/veganism-as-a-tool-for-compassion-ndgt/

Minahan, R. (2019). Tips on how to become vegan, one day at a time. Retrieved from https://www.commdiginews.com/life/tips-on-how-to-become-vegan-one-day-at-a-time-91542/

Murray-Ragg, N. (2019). 5 Tips for Transitioning to Cruelty Free and Vegan Cosmetics. Retrieved from https://www.livekindly.co/tips-cruelty-free-vegan-cosmetics/

Murray-Ragg, N. (2019). How to Find Support and Community as a Vegan | Advice | LIVEKINDLY. Retrieved from https://www.livekindly.co/finding-support-vegan/

Murray-Ragg, N. (2019). Top 10 Vegan Athletes Who Are Making Major Plant-Powered Gains. Retrieved from https://www.livekindly.co/top-vegan-athletes/

PETA. (2019). The Meat Industry Wastes Water. Retrieved from https://www.peta.org/blog/meat-industry-wastes-water/

Pevreall, K. (2019). Why Your Doctor Won't Support Your Decision to Go Vegan | LIVEKINDLY. Retrieved from https://www.livekindly.co/doctor-plant-based-nutrition/

pH-Why it Matters! - Healthy Solutions 101. (2019). Retrieved from http://healthysolutions101.com/products/33-ph-why-it-matters

Pointing, C. (2019). Can Vegans and Meat Eaters Have Lasting Relationships?. Retrieved from https://www.livekindly.co/vegan-relationships/

Pointing, C. (2019). How Do Vegans Get Enough Protein From Their Diet?. Retrieved from https://www.livekindly.co/how-do-vegans-get-enough-protein-from-their-diet/

Poultry Farming: The Shocking Reality of a Factory Farm Chicken - Sentient Media. (2019). Retrieved from

https://sentientmedia.org/poultry-farming/

ps://nutriciously.com/different-vegan-diets/

Raidt, D. (2019). How to Give Up Dairy (+ Not Miss It) | HelloGlow.co. Retrieved from https://helloglow.co/no-fail-plan-how-to-give-up-dairy-not-miss-it/

Recombinant Bovine Growth Hormone. (2019). Retrieved from https://www.cancer.org/cancer/cancer-causes/recombinant-bovine-growth-hormone.html

Rizzo, N., Jaceldo-Siegl, K., Sabate, J., & Fraser, G. (2019). Nutrient profiles of vegetarian and nonvegetarian dietary patterns. Retrieved from https://www.ncbi.nlm.nih.gov/pubmed/23988511

Rody-Mantha, B. (2019). A Complete Guide To Vegan Grocery Shopping On A Budget. Retrieved from https://thefinancialdiet.com/complete-guide-vegan-grocery-shopping-budget/

Scheler, S. (2019). 7 Tips For Switching To Cruelty-Free Products (Permanently!) ~. Retrieved from https://nanshy.com/7-tips-for-switching-to-cruelty-free-products-permanently/

Schwalfenberg, G. (2019). The Alkaline Diet: Is There Evidence That an Alkaline pH Diet Benefits Health?. Retrieved from https://www.ncbi.nlm.nih.gov/pmc/articles/PMC31955

Shields, J. (2019). If Hens Lay Eggs Anyway, Why Wouldn't Vegans Eat Them?. Retrieved from https://recipes.howstuffworks.com/why-vegans-dont-eat-eggs.htm

Simolo, G. (2019). Should You Try Vegetarianism Before Being Vegan?. Retrieved from https://www.theflamingvegan.com/view-post/Should-You-Try-Vegetarianism-Before-Being-Vegan

Simon, D. (2019). 9 Things Everyone Should Know About Farmed Fish. Retrieved from https://www.mindbodygreen.com/0-11561/9-things-everyone-should-know-about-farmed-fish.html

Skolnick, A. (2017). The CAFO Industry's Impact on the Environment and Public Health. Retrieved from https://www.sierraclub.org/sierra/2017-2-march-april/feature/cafo-industrys-impact-environment-and-public-health

Smith, K. (2019). How Bullet Journaling Can Support Your New Vegan Lifestyle (and 7 to Try) | LIVEKINDLY. Retrieved from https://www.livekindly.co/how-bullet-journaling-can-support-your-new-vegan-lifestyle-7-to-try/

Soy: The Superfood. (2019). Retrieved from https://www.psychologytoday.com/us/articles/200003

/soy-the-superfood

standard American diet | Health Topics |
NutritionFacts.org. (2019). Retrieved from
https://nutritionfacts.org/topics/standard-american-
diet/

Steen, J. (2019). HuffPost is now a part of Oath.
Retrieved from
https://www.huffingtonpost.com.au/2016/09/18/we-
found-out-if-cheese-is-really-as-addictive-as-
cocaine_a_21473133/

Striepe, B. (2019). How to Eat Vegan without Feeling
Deprived | Care2 Healthy Living. Retrieved from
https://www.care2.com/greenliving/how-to-eat-vegan-
without-feeling-deprived.html

Suddath, C. (2019). http://time.com. Retrieved from
http://time.com/3958070/history-of-veganism/

Tai Le, L., & Sabate, J. (2019). Beyond Meatless, the
Health Effects of Vegan Diets: Findings from the
Adventist Cohorts. Retrieved from
https://www.mdpi.com/2072-6643/6/6/2131/htm

The 7 Best Plant Sources of Omega-3 Fatty Acids.
(2019). Retrieved from
https://www.healthline.com/nutrition/7-plant-sources-
of-omega-3s#section8

The Alkaline Diet: An Evidence-Based Review. (2019). Retrieved from https://www.healthline.com/nutrition/the-alkaline-diet-myth#what-it-is

The Case Against Eating Fish | the kind life. (2019). Retrieved from https://thekindlife.com/blog/2018/05/the-case-against-fish/

The China Study - T. Colin Campbell Center for Nutrition Studies. (2019). Retrieved from https://nutritionstudies.org/the-china-study/

The right plant-based diet for you - Harvard Health. (2019). Retrieved from https://www.health.harvard.edu/staying-healthy/the-right-plant-based-diet-for-you

The Sad Consequences of the Standard American Diet | Atkins. (2019). Retrieved from https://www.atkins.com/how-it-works/library/articles/the-sad-consequences-of-the-standard-american-diet

The Vegan Diet and Constipation: Everything You Need to Know | Your Vegan Journey. (2019). Retrieved from https://yourveganjourney.com/the-vegan-diet-and-constipation/

Troy-Pryde, J. (2019). A Complete Beginners Guide To

Going Vegan. Retrieved from
https://www.womenshealthmag.com/uk/food/healthy-eating/a707378/vegan-diet/

Vanham, D., del Pozo, S., Pekcan, A., Keinan-Boker, L., Trichopoulou, A., & Gawlik, B. (2016). Water consumption related to different diets in Mediterranean cities. Science of the Total Environment, 573, 96-105.

Vegan For The Animals The Truth About Pigs - Epic Animal Quest. (2019). Retrieved from
http://epicanimalquest.com/blog/vegan-for-the-animals-the-truth-about-pigs/

Vegan Myth: "Animals Wouldn't Exist if We Didn't Eat Them". (2019). Retrieved from
https://www.veganlifemag.com/vegan-myth-animals-wouldnt-exist/

Vegan Myths - Don't You Need Meat To Be Healthy?. (2019). Retrieved from
https://veganuary.com/myths/dont-need-meat-healthy/

Vegan Nutrition 101: Getting All Your Nutrients on a Vegan Diet - Vegan Faux Ever. (2019). Retrieved from
https://veganfauxever.com/vegan-nutrition/

Von Alt, S. (2019). Going Out? Here's How to Find Vegan Restaurants Near You - ChooseVeg. Retrieved from https://chooseveg.com/blog/going-out-heres-how-to-find-vegan-restaurants/

Von Alt, S. (2019). Here Are 5 Vegan Meal Prep Tips for Beginners—and a Few Recipes to Try. Retrieved from https://chooseveg.com/blog/vegan-meal-prep-tips-for-beginners-and-a-few-recipes-to-try/

Von Alt, S. (2019). Pigs Are Intelligent and Sensitive, So Why Are You Eating Them?!. Retrieved from https://mercyforanimals.org/pigs-are-intelligent-and-sensitive-so-why

What Is Animal Cruelty and How Can We Stop it For Good? - Sentient Media. (2019). Retrieved from https://sentientmedia.org/animal-cruelty/

Wheeler, K. (2019). 5 Types of Vegan. Retrieved from https://happiful.com/5-types-of-vegan/

Why Eating Fish Is Even More Dangerous Than You Thought. (2019). Retrieved from https://www.mindbodygreen.com/0-12344/why-eating-fish-is-even-more-dangerous-than-you-thought.html

Wüest, F. (2019). How Vegan Diet Keeps Me Energized, Mentally Sharp and Full of Drive. Retrieved from https://www.lifehack.org/614695/how-vegan-diet-keeps-me-energized-mentally-sharp-and-full-of-drive

Made in the USA
San Bernardino, CA
08 December 2019

61106485R00115